The Ship to Nowhere

The Ship to Nowhere

On Board the *Exodus*

RONA ARATO

Second Story Press

Library and Archives Canada Cataloguing in Publication

Arato, Rona, author
The ship to nowhere : on board the Exodus / Rona Arato.

(The Holocaust remembrance series for young readers)
Issued in print and electronic formats.
ISBN 978-1-77260-018-6 (paperback).—ISBN 978-1-77260-019-3 (epub)

1. Exodus 1947 (Ship)—Juvenile fiction. 2. Holocaust, Jewish
(1939-1945)—Juvenile fiction. I. Title. II. Series: Holocaust
remembrance book for young readers

PS8601.R35S45 2016   jC813'.6   C2016-903537-9

C2016-903538-7

Editors: Sarah Silberstein Swartz and Carolyn Jackson
Copyeditor: Phuong Truong
Design: Melissa Kaita
Photo research: Gillian Robinson

Printed and bound in Canada

*The views or opinons expressed in this book and the context in which the
images are used, do not necessarily reflect the views or policy of, nor imply
approval or endorsement by, the United States Holocaust Memorial Museum.*

*Second Story Press gratefully acknowledges the support of the
Ontario Arts Council and the Canada Council for the Arts for our
publishing program. We acknowledge the financial support of the
Government of Canada through the Canada Book Fund.*

Published by
SECOND STORY PRESS
20 Maud Street, Suite 401
Toronto, ON M5V 2M5
www.secondstorypress.ca

To Rachel

PREFACE

Refugee – from the French *refugier*, "to take shelter."

The word has come to mean a person who flees to a foreign country to escape danger or persecution.

    The story of Rachel Landesman, the *Exodus 1947,* and its brave passengers and crew is especially relevant today because of the world's ongoing refugee crisis. Millions of refugees around the world continue to seek safe havens where they can live in dignity and freedom. Whether they travel on foot, in boats, rubber rafts, or other vehicles, their journeys are fraught with fear, danger, and uncertainty. These people are fleeing war, poverty, and discrimination – similar to the forces that set Rachel's story in motion after World War II. For most of the Jews of Europe trying to escape the Nazis, there was no safe haven. They had nowhere safe to go and as a result, six million people were killed just because they were Jews.

After World War II, international relief agencies set up Displaced Persons (DP) camps to help survivors. Today there are many similar refugee camps where men, women and children from war-torn countries live under terrible conditions. Like Rachel and her fellow passengers did almost 70 years ago, they wait in desperation to be accepted into a country where they can rebuild their lives. By looking to the past, we can better understand the need to help people of all religions, races, and cultures who seek a new home where they can live in peace and freedom.

PART ONE

From Europe to Palestine

CHAPTER 1
A Ship of Refugees

Sète, France, July 11, 1947

Rachel Landesman stood on the dock at Sète Harbor staring up at the ship that would take her to the land she had dreamed about: Palestine. *I am not afraid,* she told herself. But she knew she was lying. This was going to be a dangerous journey. They were boarding late at night in secret because the British, who controlled Palestine, would not allow Jews to immigrate there. She took a deep breath. The air was hot. It smelled of salt, rotting fish, and oil.

Despite her fears, Rachel's heart was filled with hope. They were leaving Europe and the horror of war behind. They were going to *Eretz Yisroel*, the ancestral land of the Jewish people. There, for the first time in their lives, they could live freely and safely as Jews.

"I don't want ever to be called a 'dirty Jew' again." Rachel didn't realize she had spoken aloud until her mother hushed her. "I'm sorry, Mama." Rachel lowered her eyes.

"It's all right." Her older sister Hensche soothed her. "You only said what we are all thinking."

"But we don't have to think out loud." Their mother gave them a stern look.

Hensche squeezed Rachel's hand. Rachel looked up at her sister. Hensche was seventeen, six years older than Rachel. She had watched over Rachel for much of her life, especially since the war ended. In the displaced persons (DP) camps where they lived after the war, it was Hensche who comforted her whenever she was sad or frightened. Usually Hensche had a sunny disposition that matched her blonde hair, but tonight her blue eyes were clouded with concern.

Rachel turned to her mother. Everyone said that she and Mama looked alike. They were both small with light brown hair and brown eyes. Rachel admired her mother who had taken them to Budapest, in Hungary, after the Nazis had invaded their own country, Czechoslovakia.

"We have made the decision to join this group and go to Palestine," Mama said. "I don't want to hear any complaints from you girls." Her mother cupped Rachel's face in her hands. "I need you to be brave."

"I will be, Mama." Rachel's eyes filled with tears. "I wish Papa were with us." Rachel barely remembered her father who had been taken from them during the war and had never returned.

"We all do." Her mother's eyes got misty, but then her expression hardened. "But we know that Papa is dead. So we have to be strong, the way he would want us to be."

"I wish Batya were here too." Rachel missed her eldest sister who had been her protector in the last months of the war. But Batya had left them to get married and she and her husband had managed to get into Palestine the previous year.

"We'll see Batya and her husband when we get to Palestine," Hensche assured her. "Don't worry, Rachel."

A young woman standing near the gangplank motioned them forward. She had big dark eyes, deeply tanned skin, and thick dark hair that she wore in a ponytail. In her blue shorts, blouse, and leather sandals, she looked different from the people boarding the ship. She looked healthy and proud. Rachel recognized her as Aviva, who had given them instructions earlier in the day. Aviva was a member of the Haganah, the Jewish Defense Force in Palestine, the group in charge of this voyage.

It was their turn to board. Rachel picked up her bundle of clothes and followed her mother and sister. Halfway up the gangplank she stopped and looked down at the dock. Hundreds of people were waiting to come on board. It was eerily quiet. Even the children seemed to sense the importance of this moment. There was no turning back.

Whatever lay ahead, Rachel thought, they were on their way to Eretz Yisroel. Taking a deep breath, she stood up straight and marched up the gangplank to the deck of the ship.

CHAPTER 2

Departure

The ship was called the SS *President Warfield*. In an effort to fool the British, who wanted to keep Jewish refugees from reaching Palestine, it was flying the flag of Honduras and pretending to head for Turkey. Everyone on board knew, however, that their true destination was Palestine. They had been told that the Jewish population was waiting to welcome them.

In all her eleven years, Rachel could not recall a time when her life hadn't been defined by the fact that she was Jewish. During the war, they had lived in constant fear of being sent to a concentration camp by the Nazis. The Nazis had killed her father. And since the end of the war, she and her mother and sister had been refugees without a home, moving from one displaced persons camp to another.

This was Rachel's first time on a ship. With so many people on board, not everyone had a place to sleep. Rachel and her family were lucky – they were assigned a bunk in the ship's hold, below deck. The hold was dark and smelly, though. People were crowded two and three to a bunk and their possessions littered the floor. Rachel walked carefully until she reached the family's bunk. It was under a porthole and by kneeling on the bunk, she could look out at the water. Exhausted, her mother and sister quickly fell asleep. But Rachel was too excited to settle down. Careful not to wake them, she climbed out of the bunk and went up to the deck.

The ship hadn't moved. They were still in the harbor. Rachel heard someone say that the French authorities had given them permission to leave the port, but would not give them a tugboat. Without a tug to guide and pull the big ship along, it couldn't get through the narrow channel and into the open sea. She looked up at the sky as it turned from black to a soft blue-gray and saw the blue Honduran flag fluttering against the emerging dawn. They had left the hotel in Sète at midnight and she had barely slept, but she was too keyed up to feel tired. *Are they going to make us go back on shore?* Rachel wondered with a sinking heart. *Please, no.*

And then the ship's horn blasted and the vessel slowly backed away from the dock.

"Rachel, what are you doing up here?"

She turned at the sound of her sister's voice. "I wanted to see what was happening." She smiled at Hensche. "This is so exciting. We didn't have a tugboat and everyone thought we'd stay in the harbor…" her words tumbled over each other. "Look." Rachel pointed to the receding shoreline. "We are leaving."

"Once and for all, I hope." Hensche turned and looked around the ship's deck. Parents were comforting tired children. A group of young people was gathered around a boy who was playing a harmonica. Two elderly men were playing chess using an overturned barrel. Everyone stopped what they were doing as a voice addressed them over a loudspeaker:

> "*Mazel tov!* Congratulations to everyone on board for making this journey. You are on a brave and important mission and I salute you. There are 4,500 people on board this ship. Each and every one of you is here for the same reason – to sail to Eretz Yisroel and a life of freedom."

The message was delivered first in Hebrew, then repeated in Yiddish and Polish. A cheer erupted from the crowd. Rachel shouted so hard her voice cracked. Hensche put an arm around her. She pointed to the golden ball of sun rising over their heads. They were out of the harbor and the water seemed to stretch forever.

"We're on our way," Rachel said, and then froze. "Hensche, look." She pointed to a British ship that had pulled alongside them.

"That's a warship," a man beside them said.

"How do you know?" Rachel asked.

"Look at the guns."

Rachel shaded her eyes to get a better look. The ship was painted a silvery gray. Its sides bristled with canons and machine guns, all pointing at them.

Others began to notice the ship. "It's a destroyer."

"They're going to attack us."

"If they do, we'll all drown!"

Everyone was pointing and shouting. So many passengers rushed over to look at the British ship that the *President Warfield* became unbalanced and tipped dangerously to one side. Rachel was caught in the crush as the ship rolled dizzyingly and the railing headed toward the water. *We're going to capsize,* she thought as she clung desperately to the rail.

"Return to your places immediately!" the captain commanded over the loudspeaker in Hebrew.

"Everyone, back to your places!" a second voice repeated in Polish and then in Yiddish.

Slowly people moved back to the main part of the deck and the ship rolled back to its upright position.

"Rachel, are you all right?" Hensche pulled her away from the rail.

"I feel sick." Rachel clapped a hand over her mouth.

"Take deep breaths."

Rachel swallowed. Her stomach was heaving and her legs felt like rubber.

"Feel better?"

Rachel nodded. She wrinkled her nose at the smell as passengers threw up over the railing. She fought off a second wave of nausea and leaned against her sister for support.

Their mother ran up to them. "These crazy people almost capsized the ship! Rachel, were you hurt?"

"Rachel had a scare." Hensche brushed wet hair off Rachel's face. "But she's fine now."

"I see we have an escort." Their mother pointed at the British ship.

Rachel turned to study the British ship again. It *was* a warship, loaded with arms that could blow them out of the water. She heard shouts and turned to see a second British destroyer on the other side of their ship.

A plane with a Union Jack – the British insignia – on its wing buzzed overhead. *We're surrounded,* Rachel thought. *We haven't fooled the British one little bit.*

CHAPTER 3
At Sea

Once the ship was underway, the Haganah leaders organized the passengers into groups. They wanted to keep people calm and occupied, to help them ignore the warships on either side of them. Rachel was assigned to a group of children on the deck and was happy that their leader was Aviva.

Although the deck was crowded, it was orderly, with people sitting in their groups. The day was sunny with a clear sky. She navigated the deck carefully, so she wouldn't step on anyone. Aviva saw her and waved her over to her group.

"Good morning, Rachel." Aviva gave her a welcoming smile. She turned to the children sitting around her. "*Yeladim,*" Aviva said, using the Hebrew word for children. Rachel had learned some Hebrew in the DP camps she had lived in for the last two years. At home they had spoken Czech and Hungarian. But she also knew Yiddish, as did most of the other Jewish children. Aviva spoke both Hebrew and Yiddish.

"Rachel, this is Miriam." Aviva introduced her to a girl about her age. "I would like the two of you to help take care of the younger children." Aviva's arm swept over the youngsters who were sitting on the deck. "Make up some games to keep them from being frightened. And bored," she added.

Rachel looked at Miriam. She was taller than Rachel and very thin, with short wheat-colored hair and blue eyes fringed with sandy lashes. "Miriam speaks Yiddish," Aviva said, "but you should both speak Hebrew as much as you can so you will become comfortable with it."

"I studied Hebrew in the camp," Rachel said. "I'll try to speak it."

"I did too," said Miriam.

"The fact that you are learning Hebrew is amazing. Do you know the story about Hebrew?" Aviva asked. When the girls shook their heads, she continued. "Hebrew was spoken in biblical times, then disappeared as a spoken language. It was the language used for prayer and study, not for everyday conversation."

"What changed?" Rachel asked, suddenly interested.

"Jews started moving back to their biblical homeland. As the Jewish population increased in Palestine, it became apparent that we needed a common language."

"What about Yiddish?" asked Rachel.

"Ashkenazi Jews from countries like Poland, Russia, and Germany speak Yiddish. But Jews from Middle Eastern countries such as Iraq, where my family is from, do not. A man named Ben Yehuda decided that we needed a common language so that Jews coming to Eretz Yisroel from all over the world could communicate. He worked hard to make Hebrew into a spoken language. Today it is the language of Jewish Palestine." She paused.

"Then that's what we will speak," Rachel said. "*Shalom*, Miriam."

"*Shalom*, Rachel," Miriam replied.

The girls continued talking in a mixture of Hebrew and Yiddish, correcting each other and giggling at their mistakes. "What should we do with them?" Miriam glanced nervously at the children who were getting restless.

"Let's lead them in singing," Rachel suggested. She turned to the group. "Who knows '*Dovid melekh yisroel*'?" she asked, naming a Hebrew song she had been taught. She began to sing and one by one, the children joined in until the air was filled with a chorus of voices and hand clapping. It was wonderful to hear the happy voices. Rachel knew that the children had all suffered. Some, like Rachel, were with parents or other family members. Others were orphans whose parents had been killed in the war. Those children were part of groups being taken to Palestine by Haganah members like Aviva.

Rachel studied the children. They came from many countries.

The handsome young captain didn't always obey the rules.

Some had lived in cities; others in villages or on farms. They spoke different languages. Some had been in concentration camps. Others had been hidden by Christian families or had lived in the forests to escape Nazi soldiers. No matter what they had experienced, they had one thing in common. *All of us,* Rachel thought, *are refugees, without a country or a home.*

"Rachel, look." Miriam pointed to Aviva who was leading a man over to their group. "That's the captain," she said in an excited voice.

Captain Ike

The man called Captain Ike was born Yitzhak Aronowicz in Danzig, Poland. His family came to Palestine in 1933, when he was ten years old. He lived with his mother, father, and three brothers in Tel Aviv. He didn't set out to become a seaman.

When he was 17, Yitzhak wanted to fight Hitler. But he didn't want to join the Jewish Brigade of the British army so he decided to go to Russia to enlist in their army. To get to Russia he tried to stow away on a ship, but was caught and sent back to Palestine. When he got home, people said he was all talk and just trying to show off. So he bribed a sailor to let him board a Palestinian ship that was sailing from Haifa to Tobruk, Libya.

After sailing on several other ships, Yitzhak went to London and completed officers' training courses and then returned to Palestine. At that time, the military defense force of Jewish Palestine was starting a naval branch but had no sailors so, with just eight months' experience at sea, Yitzhak was practically an expert. The *President Warfield* was the first ship he ever captained.

Second officer Bill Bernstein was an American who volunteered to help the Jewish refugees reach Palestine.

Aviva clapped to get everyone's attention. "Boys and girls, this is Captain Ike."

Rachel looked up in awe at the man standing before her. Captain Yitzhak Aronowitz had dark wavy hair that flopped over his forehead and a friendly smile. Like the other crewmembers he wore shorts, leather sandals, and a short-sleeved khaki shirt that showed off his muscled arms.

"That was a miracle, the way you got us out of the harbor," said a woman standing next to him.

"A miracle, no. Great seamanship, yes," said a red-haired man standing beside Captain Ike.

"So, Captain Ike. You are in charge?" asked the woman.

"No. Yossi Harel is the Haganah commander. He tells us what to do. I just sail the ship – with the help of Bill Bernstein here, the second officer," he said, clapping him on the shoulder. "I couldn't have done it without him."

"Mr. Bernstein, you are American?" the woman asked.

"Yes. I'm from New Jersey."

"And you've come all this way to help us?"

"I worked to save this rust bucket of a ship," Mr. Bernstein laughed. "I am part of a group of volunteers who salvaged and out-fitted the ship for this journey. But you can thank Captain Ike for keeping us afloat." He softened his voice. "This is a historic voyage and I am proud to be part of helping our Jewish refugees."

"Are you American too?" Rachel asked Captain Ike.

"No. I was born in Poland but I came to Palestine when I was ten and grew up there."

"Don't be so modest, Ike," the second officer said. "Tell them your story."

Captain Ike shrugged. "It is nothing special. I always loved the sea. I worked as a seaman on British ships and studied to be a captain. So," he shrugged, "when I was asked to captain this very special ship, I said yes."

"This is Ike's first time captaining a ship and he got us out of the harbor without a tug," Bill Bernstein said in a proud voice. "You are in good hands."

Captain Ike shook his head. "Now Bill is being modest. Without him, I'm not sure I could handle this ship. During the war Bill was a medical student. He could have been excused from military service. Instead he left school and volunteered for the U.S. Merchant Marines and became a second lieutenant."

"No big deal." Bill Bernstein looked embarrassed.

"Yes it is. You didn't have to fight but you did. And then," he gave him an admiring look, "he received an appointment to the United States Naval Academy at Annapolis. That is a very big deal. And do you know what this man did?"

"No," Rachel and Miriam chorused.

"He turned it down and joined the Haganah. Now he is second

officer on our ship." He looked out at the British warship and his expression darkened. "Now, if you will excuse me, I must get back up to the bridge."

"Me too." Bill Bernstein gave them a mock salute and then followed the captain.

Other crewmembers introduced themselves. Some were from Palestine, but most came from America. Rachel liked them. *With such strong, wonderful people taking care of us,* she told herself, *I know that we are in good hands.* Then she looked at the warships still surrounding them and her heart sank. *Can even the best crew in the world keep us safe from the British navy?*

CHAPTER 4

Life on Board
the Refugee Ship

When the crew left, Aviva turned her attention back to Rachel and Miriam. "If we are to live together in these crowded conditions, everyone, even children, must help keep our ship clean."

Rachel agreed. The ship was overcrowded. There weren't enough toilets or water to wash. And many people were getting sick from the rolling motion of the ship. Rachel felt hot and sweaty. Her thin cotton dress stuck to her body. But all she had to do was look at Aviva with her infectious smile and listen to her words of encouragement to keep her spirits up.

"There you are, Rachel."

Rachel looked up. "Hi, Mama. We are keeping the children happy. This is Miriam. We are partners in charge of the younger ones."

"It is nice to meet you, Miriam. When you are finished, Rachel, come down to our bunk. Your sister is waiting there and we will eat something."

Miriam watched Rachel's mother as she walked away. "You have a mother," she whispered sadly, "*and* a sister." Her blue eyes became dark.

"Oh, Miriam." Rachel took Miriam's hand. There was nothing she could say.

Hensche climbed up to the deck. It was nighttime and once again, she was looking for Rachel. She smiled to herself. Rachel was spunky and stubborn and wanted to do things her own way. During the war, Rachel had helped keep up everyone's spirits. She put on plays and even earned some money by performing for the tenants in their apartment building.

The deck was crowded and dark. Hensche had to be careful not to step on anyone as she made her way, looking for her sister. She found Rachel standing by the ship's rail talking to Aviva and Miriam.

"Mama sent me up to look for you. Why aren't you in our bunk?"

"It's so hot and smelly down there that I can't sleep." Rachel grasped the rail and leaned forward. "Hensche, I can't see the destroyer."

"That's because it's sailing without lights," Aviva explained. "Haven't you noticed? Our ship is blacked out too."

Rachel looked out into the darkness. The only light came from a sliver of moon surrounded by thousands of jeweled stars.

"It seems so peaceful." Hensche stared straight ahead. "Doesn't it?"

"For now. But I'm afraid this is the calm before the storm." Aviva looked over the deck. "This is the most crowded ship that's ever tried to get through the British blockade."

"How many ships have there been?" Rachel asked.

"Fifty, sixty."

"Did any of the people get into Palestine?"

"Not many."

Rachel felt a shiver of fear snake up her spine. "What happened to the ones who didn't make it?"

"Most of them are in refugee camps on the island of Cyprus."

Hensche frowned. "Is that what will happen to us?"

"It might. The trick is to get as many people ashore as possible once we land in Palestine, before the troops stop us," said Aviva.

"Aviva, why won't the British let us refugees into Palestine?" Rachel asked.

"It's complicated." Aviva sighed. "For 400 years, Palestine was under Turkish rule. During that time Jews, Muslims, and Christians lived there together. When the British took control of Palestine in

Conditions on board the ship were very difficult. Rachel's family had a bunk of their own, but most people had to sleep and eat on the floor of the hold below the deck, where it was hot and smelly.

1923, their government promised the Jews a homeland. They did not keep this promise. And now, in spite of the terrible things that happened to Jewish people in Europe during the war – the concentration camps, ghettos, slave labor camps, and mass murders – they still want to keep Jewish refugees out of the country."

"When the Nazis invaded Czechoslovakia, we moved to Hungary because my uncle said we would be safe there," explained Rachel.

Aviva frowned. "And you weren't." It was a statement, not a question.

Hensche broke in. "We thought we'd be better off, and at first we were. Although there were anti-Jewish laws there, Jews weren't being deported to concentration camps yet like they were in Czechoslovakia. In Hungary the men were taken to labor camps, but women, children, and older people were left alone."

"It was still pretty awful there," Rachel said. "People called us names. They spit on us. I couldn't go to school."

Aviva gave her a sympathetic look. "You don't have to talk about it."

"No, I want to. The whole world needs to know what happened to us."

CHAPTER 5
Rachel's Story

The girls and Aviva found a quiet spot on the deck and sat together as Rachel continued. "When the Nazis invaded our country, our father, like most Jewish men, was taken to a work camp. Our Hungarian uncle convinced Mama to bring the family to Budapest, but then the Nazis invaded Hungary and began rounding up Jews and sending them to concentration camps. Father escaped from his work camp and came to us in Budapest. A neighbor informed the Nazi police, the Gestapo, that he was with us. They arrested him and we never saw him again.

"One day the Gestapo came to our apartment building and ordered everyone into the courtyard. As we were being lined up, a soldier pushed me aside. Mama begged him to allow us to stay together,

Before the war, Rachel was a happy young girl, living with her family in Czechoslovakia. People said Rachel, (centre) looked like her mother (left). Hensche (right) was blonder and six years older than Rachel.

but he ignored her. Mama and Batya and Hensche were taken away with the other women. I was left all alone." Rachel paused. "I was terrified."

"Then what happened?" Miriam's voice trembled.

"I was on my own for several days until a kind neighbor took me in. A few days later, Batya managed to get away from the Nazis and return to our building. She found me in the neighbor's apartment and we stayed there. We didn't know where Mama and Hensche were. We assumed they had been deported to a concentration camp.

"One day a bomb hit our building. Batya and I escaped through the burning courtyard. We paid a Hungarian soldier to take us to the Jewish ghetto. We didn't know where else to go and at least there we would be with other Jews." Rachel's eyes filled with tears.

"You don't have to tell us more," Miriam said. She placed a hand on Rachel's shoulder.

"No. I want to. I remember...as we passed through the gate to the ghetto, the soldiers sneered and called us Jewish scum and vermin. The guard who took our identification papers glared at us. He turned to Batya and said, 'You will go here.' He handed her a paper with an address.

"As we walked to our assigned house, I saw tired, starving people. I gagged at the smell of rotting garbage. The gutters were filled with filthy water. Rats roamed the streets. Since there were no schools, children wandered aimlessly or sat listlessly on the doorsteps and curbs. They were thin and sick looking and wearing rags. I remember wondering if we would soon look like that – just because we were Jews.

"When we reached our building, we stepped into the unlit hallway and stumbled up the stairs to the second-floor apartment. It was filthy. Suddenly we heard planes overhead. The building shuddered as a bomb exploded nearby. Batya took my hand and led me down to the basement. I was terrified. We stayed there waiting for the bombing to end."

CHAPTER 6
Aviva's Story

"How were you and Batya reunited with your mother and Hensche?" Aviva asked when Rachel finished her story.

"Mama was released by the Gestapo and found us in the ghetto. She had been separated from Hensche. We didn't know what had happened to Hensche until the war ended."

"I was sent to a concentration camp," Hensche explained. "After the war, I came back to Budapest and found my mother and sisters."

"And then we were liberated from the ghetto by Russian soldiers," Rachel said. "They saved our lives."

"What about you, Aviva?" Rachel was curious. "Where were you during the war?"

"I was in Jerusalem. We heard rumors about the terrible things that were happening to Jews in Europe, but there was nothing we could do to help. After the war ended, I volunteered to go to the DP camps and help Jews get into Palestine."

"Aviva, were you born in Palestine?" Rachel asked.

"Yes. I am a Sabra. A sabra is a cactus plant that grows in Palestine," she explained. "It has a tough outer layer. But inside it is soft and sweet. That describes the Jews born in Palestine. We must be strong and tough to survive, but inside we are soft."

"Where in Palestine do you live?" Rachel asked.

"My family has lived in Jerusalem for more than a hundred years."

"Really?" Rachel was impressed.

"Yes. My great-great grandfather came from Iraq. He and my great-great grandmother had nine children, so we have a very large family. We are Mizrachi Jews – Jews who come from Arab lands." She smiled. "Mizrachi Jews speak Arabic and sometimes a language called Ladino, a mix of Arabic and Spanish."

"But you also speak Yiddish," said Miriam.

"Not very well. I learned it while I was working in the DP camps so I could communicate with people from Europe."

"How did you get into the Haganah?" asked Rachel. "Are there many other women members?"

Aviva laughed. "We are very equal in our numbers. Men and women." She thought for a moment. "I joined the Haganah because I wanted to protect our people. My aunt and uncle live on a kibbutz, a collective farm in the northern part of the country. Their kibbutz was attacked one night and Haganah members defended it. I wanted to be like them, defending our people through strength. So I joined and learned how to fight."

"Have you been on other illegal ships like this?" asked Miriam.

"This is my third."

"What will happen when we get to Palestine?" Hensche asked.

"The plan is for Captain Ike to run the ship up on the beach in Tel Aviv. You will get off and mix with the hundreds of people who will be waiting on the beach. With people running every which way, the soldiers will catch some of you, but many will get away."

Hensche frowned. "And what happens if we don't even make it to Tel Aviv?"

Aviva turned back to the sea. "Soon we will be in Palestinian territorial waters."

"What does that mean?" Hensche asked.

"It means that we will be in a part of the sea that belongs to Palestine." At Rachel's puzzled look, she continued. "A country has the right to control the ocean up to 22 kilometers, or about 12 miles, from its shore. The rest of the ocean is international. That means that ships from any country can sail there. Since the British rule Palestine, they control that part of the sea known as Palestinian waters."

Rachel digested this new fact. "Will they attack us when we are in Palestinian waters?"

Jews were forced to wear yellow stars that identified them.

"I don't know what they *will* do, however I am afraid of what they *might* do. But don't worry. We are ready to fight."

Rachel watched Aviva walk away. *She is so sure of herself, so confident and proud.* "I wish I were a Sabra. They are so…" Rachel searched for a word, *"free."* The word popped into her head like a burst of music. "They live in a country where they are proud to be Jews. They haven't lived in hiding or had to wear yellow stars."

CHAPTER 7
New Friends

Tension on the ship was mounting. They were in the part of the Mediterranean Sea that was considered international water. Yet they were surrounded by a fleet of British warships and threatened by planes buzzing overhead.

Rachel overheard two men talking as she came up on deck in the morning. "They are going to attack us. Why else would they send the whole British navy?" The ship was now 20 nautical miles (40 kilometers) from the shore of Palestine.

"We are still in international waters. They can't attack us here," said a man watching the four British warships surrounding them.

"As if that matters to them. So, let them attack," the other man responded. "We will fight back."

"With what?" asked the first man.

"Our bare hands, if necessary." He punched the air with his fists.

Rachel whirled around to them. "We'll fight, if we have to."

Two boys standing close by looked at her in amazement. "*We?* Really?" The first boy gave her a bemused look. "And where did you learn to fight?" He was speaking Yiddish.

"I, I didn't. But I will. What about you?"

"I *do* know how to fight. I fought with the partisans against the Nazis in Poland."

Rachel looked at him in awe. Partisans were heroes. They were people who escaped from the Nazis and hid in the forests and fought back. She looked closely at the young boy who looked her age. "Did you really fight?"

The boy puffed out his chest. "I blew up a train track." He held out his hand. "I'm Saul Cohen. This fellow," he pointed at his friend, "is David Solomon."

Rachel studied the boys. Saul was thin with green eyes and a mop of curly red hair. He wore navy blue shorts and a white shirt. David was shorter than Saul with dark brown hair and eyes and a friendly smile. He wore wire-rimmed glasses and was dressed like Saul, only his shorts were khaki-colored.

"You look awfully young to be partisans. How old are you?"

"We're fourteen." Saul straightened his shoulders. "I helped the people who blew up train tracks in Poland."

"What did you do for them?"

"He carried water," David said. He placed a hand on Saul's shoulder. "We both did. They said we were too young to fight, but we helped those who did."

"We did more than carry water. We helped string the wire for the bombs." Saul rubbed his chin. "We lived in the woods and kept moving, so the Nazi soldiers wouldn't find us. In the winter, it was freezing. It was summer when we joined the group and we didn't have warm clothes. Some of the members gave us things to wear, but nothing ever fit. We slept outdoors. Sometimes we found a deserted house and slept there. We never had enough food."

"At least we were free," David interrupted. He took off his glasses, wiped the lens on his shirt. "That's better," he said as he put them back on. "It wasn't easy living in the forest but at least we weren't taken to concentration camps in cattle cars."

Saul's expression darkened. "Like the rest of our families."

CHAPTER 8
Saul's Story

"What happened to your family?" Rachel asked Saul.

"I'm from a town called Plotzk," said Saul. "It's in the middle of Poland, on the Vistula River, not far from Warsaw. There were 9,000 Jews living there before the war, more than one-quarter of the town's population. When the war started, many Jews left Plotzk and went east to Russia. My father was taken to a work camp and my mother thought the Nazis wouldn't hurt the women and children, so we stayed in the ghetto. But conditions got much worse. They closed our schools, took away Jewish businesses, and destroyed our Great Synagogue. They made us wear patches with Jewish stars and humiliated Jews by cutting off their beards. In February 1941, they rounded up the remaining Jews and began sending them to concentration camps.

When the Nazis came to our house, I was in the woods, searching for wood to burn in our stove. By the time I got back, everyone was gone."

"How did you end up with the partisans?" Rachel asked.

"I hid in a shed behind our house and waited until it was dark. Then I ran back to the woods. I had heard about a group of Jews who were living in the forest. I had to be careful because some of the local people were turning Jews over to the Nazis. Other Polish friends and neighbors," he said in a bitter voice, "were too afraid to help us."

Saul took a deep breath. "After dark, I walked to the forest. I slept there that night and the next morning one of the men from the partisan camp found me. I stayed with them for the rest of the war. That's where I met David."

"How did you get there, David?" Rachel asked.

"I had escaped from Plotzk into the country with my parents before Jews were sent to the camps," explained David. "Then my father was shot. That winter my mother got sick and died."

"So David and I adopted each other." Saul said. "When the war was over, we went back to Plotzk because we hoped we'd find some family. When I went to our house there were new people living in it. They told me that if I was still there in the morning they would kill me. I couldn't believe it. These people had been our neighbors before the war."

"I wasn't welcomed back either," David said. "So we went to a refugee center in Warsaw and they sent us to a DP camp in Germany."

"You were both very brave," Rachel looked at them with respect.

They stopped talking as Aviva marched up to them. "What are all of you doing standing around when there is so much work to be done? Rachel, Miriam is waiting for you to help with the young ones. David, Saul, come with me."

CHAPTER 9
Miriam and Rachel

After they finished helping with the younger children, Rachel and Miriam found a spot on the deck where they could sit and talk. It was noon and the ship was bathed in sunshine. Rachel wore white shorts and a red-and-white checked blouse that Hensche had sewn for her. The blouse had buttons shaped like daisies and Rachel fingered these as she talked.

"How did you end up on this ship?" Rachel asked Miriam.

Miriam wrapped her arms around her knees and pulled them to her chest. "We lived in Paris. My father owned a coat factory just outside the city. When the Nazis started rounding up Jews, Papa took me to the home of a man who worked for him. He and his wife took me in. Their name was Gerard." She patted her blonde hair. "They told people I was their niece and that my parents were killed when the Germans invaded France. I lived with them for four years."

"Were they good to you?"

"Yes. They treated me like a daughter. They taught me how to be a good Catholic girl so the neighbors wouldn't suspect I was Jewish. I went to church and learned all the prayers. I almost forgot that I *am* Jewish." She looked around the ship. "But I always remembered what my father told me. He said to pretend I was Christian, but never to forget who I really am.

Rachel and her sister and mother stayed with the nuns in this German convent for a year after the war ended.

"After the war, I waited for my parents to come for me, but they never did. From some family friends, I found out that they'd died in the Auschwitz concentration camp. The Gerards wanted to keep me in their home, but I remembered what my father said about being true to who I am. So Madame Gerard took me to a Jewish orphanage. A man came there to speak to us. He told us that the best place for a Jew to live was Eretz Yisroel and that he would take us there. And so, here I am on this ship." She gave Rachel a weak smile. "That is my story. How did you get here?"

"I hated being Jewish in Hungary. I always felt like an outsider. I watched Jews being beaten and arrested. I heard people talk about Eretz Yisroel and I decided that it was the only place I wanted to live."

"When did you leave Budapest?"

"A few months after the war ended. We were in a several DP camps. The best was a convent in Holthhausen, Germany. The nuns were very kind to us. We worked in the fields and there was always food."

"Why did you leave?"

"We were there for more than a year and the nuns asked us to leave. So we went to the Hochland DP camp near Fohrenwald in Germany. It is a small camp that was run as a kibbutz, and we learned agriculture. But we didn't stay there long. My mother wanted me to go to school, so we went to a town."

"But how did you end up on this ship?" asked Miriam.

"Mama enrolled me in a Jewish school where they talked about Eretz Yisroel. I told my mother that we should live in Eretz Yisroel."

"And you still say that." Her mother came up to them. "Rachel is as stubborn as a mule."

"And I'm proud of it." Rachel sprang to her feet. "Mama, this is what we all want now."

"Yes, darling, we all want to arrive in Palestine." Her mother gave her an amused smile. "It's just that not everyone is as vocal about it as you are."

CHAPTER 10
The Star of David Rises

July 17, 1947

The ship had been sailing for six days and was almost in Palestinian waters. It was still surrounded by British warships and everyone now believed that the British would attack as soon as they left the international zone. Their hope was that Captain Ike would sail the ship at top speed and run it up onto the beach in Tel Aviv where the Haganah would help refugees "disappear" into the masses of Jewish Palestinians waiting for them.

At three o'clock, the Haganah leaders gathered all the passengers on the upper deck. It was so crowded that sitting was impossible. Everyone stood, shoulder to shoulder, facing the bridge where Captain Ike and his crew stood looking down on them. Some

The *Exodus 1947*

The *Exodus 1947* started life as the SS *President Warfield*, a luxury steamboat that toured the Chesapeake Bay between Maryland and Virginia in the United States. It was built to carry 300 passengers who enjoyed the scenery, entertainment, and good food aboard. During World War II, it was loaned to the British navy and, in 1944, took part in the Allied invasion of Normandy, the event known as D-Day.

The ship returned to the United States battered from its wartime service, fit only for scrap metal. In a secret operation, agents from the Haganah bought and refitted the ship to hold 4,500 refugees with $40,000 raised from North American Jews. The ballroom was ripped out and replaced with wooden slabs for bunks. The ship was outfitted with food, blankets, medical supplies, and life jackets. The lower decks were covered with nets and barbed wire to keep British soldiers from boarding.

The SS President Warfield

passengers had brought their suitcases, as if preparing to disembark. Others were busy piling stacks of "ammunition" that they could throw at the soldiers. Cans of food, potatoes, onions, and iron bars were spread along the sides of the deck. When everyone was assembled, Yossi Harel, the Haganah commander, called them to order. Rachel stared at him. With his dark hair and handsome face he reminded her of a movie star. And when he spoke, his voice commanded attention.

The *President Warfield* left Baltimore on February 25, 1947. Because its mission was secret, it sailed under a flag from the Republic of Honduras and pretended its destination was China. The ship hit a brutal storm. It took on water and the crew feared it would sink. They sent out an SOS and were rescued by the American Coast Guard. When newspapers printed the story of the rescue, reporters started asking questions. If the ship was sailing under a Honduran flag and was supposed to be going to China, why was it carrying maps and charts of the Mediterranean Sea?

Most of the crew left after the storm – they did not believe the ship was seaworthy. The new crew consisted of young Jewish American volunteers who were sworn to secrecy. They could not tell anyone, not even their parents, where they were going or why. None of them had sailing experience. On March 29, 1947, after extensive repairs, the *President Warfield* left Baltimore for Marseilles, France. However, the British were suspicious and tracked its movements. To confuse them, the crew sailed to Italy, then back to the port of Sète, France where the refugees came on board and the *President Warfield* sailed into troubled waters as *Exodus 1947*.

"We believe that the British will try to board our ship as soon as we're in Palestinian waters. We have done everything we can to keep them off. But if they succeed, we are going to fight them with all our might. We will not let them take control!" He was interrupted by loud cheers from the crowd. "When I tell you to fight," he continued, "I mean with no knives or firearms. We do not want to kill British soldiers. We do not want British blood on our hands. Now," he said, "let us get organized."

Suddenly there was a commotion on the bridge. Everyone looked up. Two crewmembers were lowering the Honduran flag. As the passengers watched in awe, they replaced it with the blue-and-white Star

Yossi Harel

Yossi Harel was born in Jerusalem where his family had lived for six generations. He joined the Haganah when he was 15. During World War II he fought for the British. After the war he commanded four refugee ships, carrying 25,000 Holocaust survivors trying to get into Palestine. The most famous was the *Exodus 1947*, which Yossi named.

The character Ari Ben Canaan in the book *Exodus*, by Leon Uris, was based on Yossi Harel. Paul Newman played him in the 1960 film version of the book.

of David, the six-pointed star that had been the symbol of the Jewish people, since biblical times.

Rachel caught her breath. "Look, Hensche. We have our own flag."

"It's beautiful," Hensche sighed. She turned to the side of the ship where other crewmembers were hanging a sign on the rail.

"What does it say?" Rachel moved forward to get a better look. Draped over the top deck railing was a sign that read: "*Haganah Ship Exodus 1947.*" Their ship had been renamed by the crew, based on Jewish history – the exodus from Egypt, where they had been slaves.

All around them people were cheering. A short man looked at Rachel, his eyes glistening. "Pay attention, young lady. This is a historic moment. We are on a momentous journey. That flag will be the symbol of our new country." He walked away, urging others to celebrate.

"Our country! Hensche, did you hear that?"

"Do you know who that man is?" Saul watched as the man worked his way through the exuberant crowd. "It's Mordecai Rosman. He was a hero with the partisans in the forest."

Rachel's head was reeling. There was a new flag. Their ship was now called *Exodus 1947.* She had seen Mordecai Rosman, whom Saul called a hero. And she had listened to Yossi Harel, the Haganah commander in charge of their ship.

"Rachel." Hensche took her arm. "Come, let's find Mama."

Rachel's attention turned back to her sister. They walked across the deck. The organizers had divided it into sections and everyone was ordered to stay with his or her own group. Her family was assigned to the left, the port side of the ship. As she followed her sister, she looked out to sea. The warships seemed to be closer than ever. She studied the sailors lining the deck. *What are they thinking? Are they frightened? Do they want to attack us or would they rather let us reach our destination?*

Their mother was seated in their assigned section.

"Aviva says that if the British attack, they will send us to a camp on Cyprus," Rachel said.

"At least it will be warmer than it was in Germany," Hensche observed wryly.

"What's it like on Cyprus?" Rachel asked her sister.

"I don't know, but it's in the Mediterranean Sea." Hensche pointed to the sky, ablaze with afternoon sunshine.

Suddenly the ship pitched, like a horse going over a fence. Rachel stumbled, regained her balance and then plopped down next to her mother. Hensche squeezed into the narrow space between them. The ship righted itself and, in clear view of the British destroyer, they settled in to wait for whatever would happen next.

When the ship was getting close to Palestine, the crew hoisted the Star of David flag and renamed the ship Haganah Ship Exodus 1947.

CHAPTER 11

Waiting

The refugee ship called Exodus 1947 *is headed for the shores of Palestine, after having succeeded in breaking through the blockade upon emigration from ports of exit. The Haganah ship…has 4,554 refugees: 1,600 men, 1,282 women, 1,017 young people, 655 children. The ship has been spotted by the British navy. A naval force, five destroyers and a cruiser, are now closing in on her from all sides, and leading her on her way.*[1]

—From a handbill posted by Haganah youth
in Tel Aviv, Jerusalem, Natanya, and Haifa.

Lunch on deck was over and they had returned to their bunks in the hold. Rachel sat on the edge of the bed listening to the instructions broadcast through the loudspeaker.

"Tonight we'll arrive at the coast of Palestine. *Exodus* passengers, please stay in your bunks and wait for further instructions. Be dressed and ready to leave the ship when it reaches the Palestine shore."

The afternoon dragged on as the passengers waited in silence. Rachel's mind whirled with questions. *We are going to Tel Aviv, but will the British allow us to get off the ship?*

A woman's voice from an upper bunk echoed her thoughts. "I was in Bergen Belsen, the concentration camp liberated by the British. They saved my life and now, two years later, I'm their enemy? Does this make sense?"

"Shah, Eva," a soft voice responded. "We survived the war and the camps. We will survive this too."

"How many times must we survive before we can just live?" said the first woman.

The cabin became silent. Rachel felt the mounting tension. She looked out the porthole. The light was fading as afternoon turned to evening. The air was stifling. She jumped from the bed.

"What are you doing?" her mother demanded.

"I'm going up on deck. I want to find out what's happening. I'm going to find Aviva."

"Rachel, we need to stay together."

"I'll be back, Mama. I promise." She raced to the stairs and climbed up to the deck before anyone could stop her.

❀ ❀ ❀

Night had fallen and the upper deck was dark. As before, the ship was blacked out, as were the British warships. When Rachel's eyes adjusted, she saw that the deck was full of people. Some were clutching their belongings, ready to leave the ship at any moment. Others were guarding the piles of cans, wooden sticks, iron bars, and other things that people called ammunition, stacked along the sides of the deck. Her heart was pounding. *Why did I come up? I should be with my mother. I want my sister.* She turned to go back. Before she could move, a strong beam of light blinded her. A voice over a loudspeaker blasted a message from the British warship:

"*Exodus* passengers, your ship is entering Palestinian waters. From now on, you must obey our orders!"

"Let them try to make us leave!" a voice cried out.

"We'll fight to the last person!" shouted another.

All around her, men and women called out, whistling and jeering. Saul appeared at her side.

"I'm ready to fight." He held up balled fists.

"Where is David?" Rachel asked.

"Over there." Saul pointed to a group stacking food cans along the side of the ship. "I'm going to help them. Stay safe." He gave Rachel an encouraging smile and left.

Rachel covered her ears. The noise was deafening as people shouted to drown out the message from the warship, which was being repeated over and over. Then, as suddenly as had it appeared, the light went out, the message stopped, and the night plunged back into darkness and silence.

"Rachel, here you are." Her mother's voice was worried. "I couldn't find you."

"I wanted to know what was happening, Mama."

"We have brought all our clothes up on deck. From now on, we stay together!"

An eerie quiet settled over the crowded deck. Rachel searched the darkness but couldn't see the British ships. *Maybe this time, they'll go away and leave us alone,* she thought. But deep inside, she knew that her wish was futile.

Then everything happened at once.

CHAPTER 12
The Attack

Pre-dawn, July 18, 1947

Night turned to day. A warship, lit up from stem to stern, pulled alongside the *Exodus*. Through the glare, Rachel saw armed soldiers lining the ship's deck. And then an object flew through the air. *Thwack!* A canister landed at her feet and she was engulfed in a cloud of fumes. Her eyes burned and she felt as if she were choking. More canisters rained down, filling the air with poisonous gray smoke. All around her people were coughing and begging for help.

"Tear gas! They are using tear gas on us!" someone called out.

"Help me," cried a woman. "My eyes are burning! I can't see!"

Rachel stumbled blindly, searching for her mother and sister. "Mama! Hensche!"

"I'm here, Rachel." Hensche grabbed her hand.

Rachel blinked hard and after a moment, the deck came into a misty focus. People were crying and screaming. A group of young men and women had gathered at the ship's rail and were throwing cans, potatoes, and onions down at the deck of the warship. And, above all the noise, the *Exodus'* siren wailed without pause. And then, as suddenly as it began, the tear gas attack stopped, the lights on the British ship went out and the *Exodus* was again dark.

"How can they use gas on Jews!" A man beside Rachel held his head in his hands.

"What does he mean?" Rachel looked questioningly at her mother.

"In the concentration camps, the Nazis used gas to kill Jews." Her voice broke.

"A different gas," the man who had spoken explained. "This," he pointed to his eyes, "is tear gas. It won't kill us. Still…" His voice was drowned out by the wailing siren. "Turn that thing off!"

"The siren is broken. Please, everyone. Stay calm," Aviva's voice commanded.

"Are you all right?" Rachel turned to her mother and Hensche.

"I think so. The smoke," Hensche clutched her throat and coughed. "I felt like I was choking."

"I did too." Rachel rubbed her eyes. They were still burning from the tear gas fumes. Someone handed her a wet rag.

"Put it over your eyes. It will make them feel better."

Rachel put the rag over her eyes. The soggy cotton eased the burning. She tried to relax, but her brain felt as sore as her eyes. *I want to believe that we are going to Palestine. We are almost there!* In spite of the attack, the *Exodus* was still plowing through the water.

Rachel heard a loud crash as a sharp jolt sent her tumbling forward. "We've been hit," someone shouted as the ship tilted to one side. The ammunition that had been stockpiled was rolling everywhere. Rachel was on her hands and knees, searching for something to hold on to. She heard screams coming from the lower deck. She twisted her neck, frantically searching for Mama and Hensche.

"We're here, Rachel!" Her mother pulled her to her feet.

It was hard to stand on the sloping deck, but Rachel managed to find her balance. She stared into the darkness, searching for the warship. It was gone. Relief, however, was short-lived, as a second ship slammed the *Exodus* from the other side and passengers were once again bombarded with tear gas.

"Are we going to sink?" Rachel looked around fearfully. Gray smoke from the tear gas clouded the night air. People were screaming and crying. Mothers clutched their children. She saw men helping people climb out of the damaged hold. Many were injured.

"Are you hurt?" Suddenly Miriam was at her side.

"No. Are you?"

"Only in here." Miriam put her hand over her heart.

The girls clung to each other. Then Rachel straightened. She looked around the shattered deck and lifted her head. "They haven't beaten us, Miriam. Whatever happens, don't let the soldiers see us cry."

"That's the spirit, little girl!" A man with blood streaming down his face patted her on the shoulder. "Keep your spirits up. You too," he said to Miriam.

"I'll try," she responded. She looked at her friend. Rachel's face was calm. Her eyes shone with determination. "She's so brave," Miriam thought. "I will be too."

CHAPTER 13

The Battle

Morning, July 18, 1947

This is the refugee ship Exodus 1947. *Before dawn today, we were attacked by five British destroyers and one cruiser at a distance of seventeen miles from the shores of Palestine, in international waters. The assailants immediately opened fire, threw tear gas bombs, and rammed our ship from three directions. On our deck, there are one dead, five dying, and a hundred-twenty wounded. The resistance continued for more than three hours. Owing to the severe losses and the condition of the ship, which is in danger of sinking, we were compelled to sail in the direction of Haifa, in order to save the 4,500 refugees on board from drowning.*[2]

—Voice of John Stanley Grauel, crewmember, transmitted on
The Voice of Israel radio station, July 18, 1947

The two British warships had rammed into both sides of the *Exodus*. The results were catastrophic. Water flooded into the ship and the passengers feared that it was sinking. But somehow, the *Exodus* managed to stay afloat.

Then the British attacked again. Some managed to board, but a group of young refugees pushed them off. There were loud splashes as the British sailors fell into the water. After a few minutes, the British ship sailed off and an uneasy calm descended. But not for long.

Captain Ike and his second officer, Bill Bernstein looked down at the deck. "We can't win a battle with the British if they board us," the captain said.

"I have a premonition," the second officer replied. "I don't think I will survive this battle."

"Don't say that." Captain Ike placed a hand on his shoulder. "You will come through this. We all will."

"We can't win this battle," Bill's eyes clouded over. "If I don't survive, at least I will have died fighting for my people."

As he finished speaking the warship returned and this time British soldiers scaled up rope ladders they attached to the side of the *Exodus*. They climbed onto the deck. Then the real battle began.

Rachel sat on her bunk listening to the fighting above. Hensche had gone upstairs to the deck, but her mother held Rachel back.

"One fighting daughter is enough. Stay here out of trouble."

Rachel sulked.

"Oh!" Mama put her face in her hands. She sat on the bunk rocking back and forth as sounds of the fight funneled down the stairs and into the hold. "They will be killed," she moaned.

Rachel couldn't stand not knowing what was going on. She jumped up. "I'm going on deck!" She wrested out of her mother's grasp, dashed to the stairs, and bounded up to the deck. Soldiers were beating the passengers with truncheons, clubbing people on their backs, arms, and heads. The passengers fought back, throwing anything they could find. Rachel saw Hensche wielding a stick. She looked for David and Saul. As she expected, they were in the thick of the fight. She searched for something to throw and saw a potato rolling across the deck. She grabbed it and was about to toss it at a soldier when she heard gunshots.

CHAPTER 14
Surrender

The battle was over. Dawn was breaking as the *Exodus*'s loudspeaker crackled to life.

"*Exodus* passengers, stop your fighting!"

Heads turned toward the bridge. A cloud of gloom settled over the ship as the message sank in. The *Exodus* had lost the fight for now. More British soldiers came aboard.

The ship was in shambles. It was leaning badly to one side. The deck was littered with debris and many people were injured. Rachel found Hensche, who was thankfully unharmed. Nearby she saw a man on

*Once morning came, the passengers could
see the amount of damage to the ship.*

a stretcher, his head wrapped in a bloody bandage. Injured passengers were sprawled on the deck as British medics moved through the crowd, tending to their wounds. She saw Aviva near the front of the ship surrounded by a group of children and ran to her.

"The fight was awful! So many people are hurt. Are you all right?"

"Yes, I am, but Bill Bernstein is dead."

Rachel looked at her in stunned silence.

"What happened?" a woman behind her asked.

"They beat him with clubs." Aviva's voice shook.

"Oy!" The woman covered her face with her hands. "Such a wonderful man. He didn't have to come here from America to help us. But he did."

"Those monsters," said a man next to her.

"Many people are hurt." Aviva looked around the deck. People were reacting angrily to the news of Bill Bernstein's death. Two other people, including a young boy, had been killed. The crowd was furious at the British for launching the attack and sad for the people killed and injured.

"What will happen now?" Rachel asked Aviva in a frightened voice.

"They will send you to Cyprus." Her expression became wary. "Rachel, watch the children. I must go."

"Is she part of the Haganah?" a soldier asked as Aviva melted into the crowd. "No," he held up a hand. "Better don't tell me." At Rachel's puzzled look, he explained. "The Haganah organized this illegal transport and our soldiers are supposed to arrest them. But don't worry." He patted her shoulder. "I'm sure they can take care of themselves."

Rachel didn't understand his words but she recognized his gestures. She looked to where Aviva had disappeared and smiled.

❀ ❀ ❀

"Were you in the fight?" Saul asked Rachel. His face was smudged and his right eye looked like a purple eggplant.

"No, but I see that you were."

"I hit a soldier's head with a can of peaches. I really hurt him."

"Good for you. How is David?"

Saul winced as he tried to talk through swollen lips. "They beat him pretty hard. The medics are taking care of him."

"Will he be all right?" Rachel gave him a worried look.

"I hope so." He looked worried. "David is tough. He survived in the forest and he'll survive now." Saul shook his head. "We put up a good fight."

"You did." Rachel saw her own regret mirrored in his eyes.

Hensche came up to them. "Rachel, Mama is looking for you."

"Take care of that eye, Saul." She followed Hensche to their mother who was showing identification papers to another soldier. "This is my other daughter, Rachel," she said as Rachel joined them.

The soldier checked their papers and moved on to another group.

"Always with the papers," said Mama. "Are we legal? Illegal? What we are is refugees."

Her mother and Hensche had brought all their belongings up on deck. After the soldier left, they started putting on all their clothes.

British soldiers came on board to check the identification documents of the refugees.

"What are you doing?" Rachel looked at them in confusion.

"We are going to wear everything we own. And you have to do the same."

"Everything?" Rachel asked, looking at the mound of sweaters, skirts, and blouses piled on the deck.

"Yes. We don't want to leave anything behind."

"Why can't we just carry them?"

"This way the soldiers can't take them from us."

"Listen to Mama!" Hensche said in a weary voice.

Rachel looked at her sister who was wearing a coat with a fur collar over layers of dresses. Her face was flushed from the heat and tendrils of blonde hair clung to her face. Her mother too was weighed down with skirts, blouses, and sweaters. Rachel sighed and started pulling on clothes. "I feel like a barrel," she said, looking down at herself. "It's so hot."

The fighting had taken place at night but now it was morning. Sunlight sparkled on the water. Seagulls circled overhead. Their loud squawks were a welcome sound after the angry roar of British warplanes. The *Exodus* was now in Palestinian waters. In the distance, Rachel saw the hills of Haifa. The hills grew bigger as the ship was led to the port of Haifa. White dots became houses, where people ate, slept, celebrated, and lived their lives. Rachel stared at them with a longing so strong she thought her heart would break.

CHAPTER 15

Response in Tel Aviv

July 18, 1947

The citizens of Tel Aviv reacted angrily to news of the ramming of the *Exodus*. "Why won't you let our people land!" they shouted. Signs bearing this slogan appeared on windows and billboards all over the city, as well as in Jerusalem, Netanya, and Haifa. On Friday, July 18, the citizens declared a general strike. People closed their shops and restaurants. They turned off machinery in factories. Crowds filled the streets, protesting the actions of the British. By ten o'clock that morning, the entire city of 200,000 people had stopped all activity to protest the treatment of the refugees on the ship. Hotels were blacked out. Cafes closed. A sign was posted on the beach that said there would be no swimming.

An American journalist, Ruth Gruber, walked among the crowd. People were angry. She heard them screaming:

"Maybe my father is on board."
"My sister must surely be coming."

Ruth Gruber was very sympathetic toward the refugees. She had been in the DP camps in Europe after the war and had reported on the terrible conditions of people desperate to find a new home and begin new lives. The refugees had survived the ghettos and Nazi death camps and now they were being turned away from the one country in the world that they hoped would be open to them.

When the *Exodus* wasn't allowed to land in Tel Aviv, she drove to Haifa by car. Every few miles, she was stopped at barbed wire checkpoints and questioned by British soldiers. When she finally reached Haifa, she went directly to the dock. The Haifa harbor was filled with fishing boats. Nothing moved. It was as if the entire port of Haifa was holding its breath waiting to see what would happen.

Ruth Gruber stood on the pier with the other reporters. A wall of soldiers separated them from the dock where the *Exodus* would be arriving. They were warned that anyone caught talking to the refugees would be expelled from the port.

There were three ships tied up at the pier. Ruth looked with horror at the barbed wire and steel mesh cages on the deck of each ship.

She looked out to sea. The *Exodus* suddenly became visible on the horizon, plowing through the choppy water, surrounded by British destroyers. The blue-and-white flag with the Star of David fluttered from its flagpole.

CHAPTER 16
Arrival in Haifa

*The enemy came in slowly, a black, shabby broken steamer
pulled into place by British tugs. She had a single tall black
funnel. Fore and aft, the blue-and-white flag of Zion flew
from her masts. We saw her name clearly now:* Haganah Ship
Exodus 1947.

*The voices of thousands of people [aboard the ship] floated
to us on the quay. They were singing "Hatikvah", the Hebrew
hymn of hope. It was the song the Jews sang at every emergency
and in every crisis. It was their song of survival.*[3]

—Ruth Gruber

As the *Exodus* approached the Haifa shore, its passengers gazed out to the land that they hoped would become home. At about four o'clock in the afternoon, a pair of tugboats pulled the ship into port. *They wouldn't give us tugboats to leave France*, Rachel thought, *but now they are using them to tow us into Haifa.*

Rachel expected to see Haifa residents crowding the dock to welcome them as they were told had happened at the beaches of Tel Aviv. Instead, their greeting committee consisted of rows of soldiers in red berets, armored vehicles sprouting machine guns, and military ambulances. Coils of rusted wire covered the pier. She later learned that no one except the British army, navy, and some press was allowed in the port of Haifa to meet the ship. As the *Exodus* settled into its berth, a loudspeaker from the pier blasted a message: "The commanding officer wishes you to come off quietly, women and children first."

Soldiers placed gangplanks against the ship and then climbed on board. Some carried stretchers. *Will they carry David on one of those stretchers?* Rachel wondered. She was frantic to find out what had happened to her friend. So many people were hurt. Three were dead and others in danger of dying. *Once we're on shore I'll find out what happened to David. I hope he's all right. Saul will know.*

Rachel turned her gaze to the shore. Haifa was beautiful. She looked longingly at the rows of buildings climbing up Mount Carmel. She could make out streets with trees and shops. It was Friday. People were getting ready for Shabbat. *If we lived here, I would be helping*

Mama make dinner. We would set the table and light candles and have roast chicken and maybe strudel for dessert. In her daydream, her father was with them sitting around a table, set with a crisp white cloth.

As twilight approached, Rachel looked up at the slope of the mountain with all its little lights. She knew that for the rest of her life she would remember those blinking lights on Mount Carmel.

Tugboats and a fireboat guided the Exodus 1947 *into Haifa harbor. As the ship approached, its passengers gazed out at the British soldiers and armored tanks assembled on the dock. Those on the dock could see the amount of damage done to the ship and its 4,500 passengers standing on the deck.*

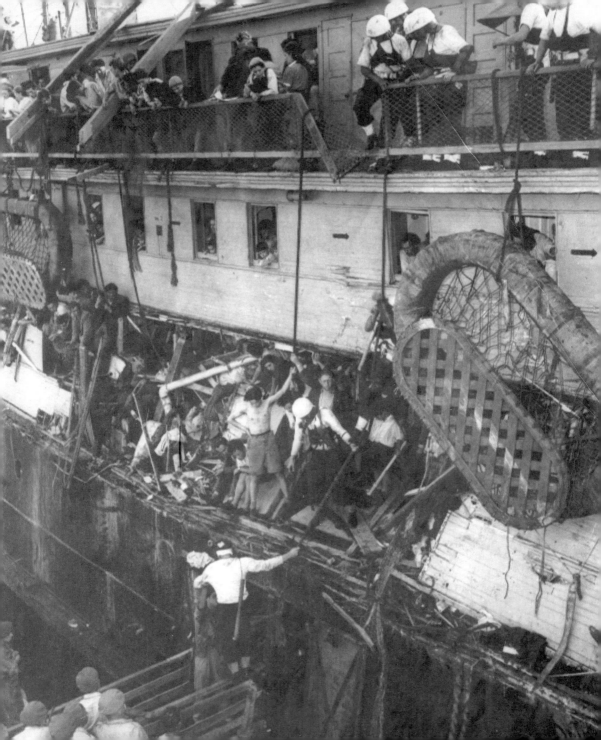

CHAPTER 17
Where Next?

The refugees began their descent. "This is all I have in the world! You can't take it from me!" a woman screamed as a soldier collected her baggage.

"You will be going to Cyprus, ma'am. You will get everything back once we are there." He handed her a large sticker and showed her where to put her name.

"At least we still have our clothes," her mother said.

"It's too hot wearing everything," Rachel complained.

"I don't trust them." Her mother gave the soldier a sideways glance. "Better we should keep everything with us."

Rachel wrapped her arms around her chest. "I feel like I'm wearing armor."

"Listen to Mama," Hensche mouthed.

As they waited their turn to disembark, Rachel studied the faces of the other passengers. Some looked resigned. Others were angry. Everyone looked tired. Soldiers were everywhere on the ship and on the dock. They herded people down the gangplank, tossing about the passengers' belongings.

The casualties had been taken off the ship and put into ambulances. There were so many wounded, mostly young men, in bloodied shirts, some with heads wrapped in bandages. Rachel watched them, hoping to see David.

"Rachel." Her mother tugged her arm. "It is our turn." Silently they followed the soldiers leading them across the deck and down the gangplank.

Behind them, the ship rested like a wounded animal. Until now, Rachel hadn't realized how much damage it had sustained. She could see into the cabin, to the remains of bunks. The walls of the promenade deck were splintered so that shards of wood protruded like broken matchsticks. There was an enormous hole in the center of the hull exposing mounds of crumpled bedding, broken pipes, and passengers' scattered belongs. The cabins were smashed in. It was a miracle that the ship hadn't broken into pieces and sunk. *But it remained afloat*, she thought, *and we survived. Now we must survive whatever comes next.*

The British soldiers were standing at attention, guns on their shoulders. Ahead was an enormous tent. The line of passengers inched forward. They stopped at the tent entrance. The boy in front of them was arguing with a soldier.

"You can't take that knife," the boy protested. "It's mine." He tried to pull the knife out of the soldier's hand.

"Sorry, son, this isn't allowed," the soldier said as he deposited the penknife into a large box. "Move along," he waved. "Next!"

Still grumbling, the boy marched into the tent. Now it was their turn.

"Hands up, please. I have to search you." He motioned for them to raise their arms.

"For what?"

"Weapons." The soldier smiled. "You might have a cannon hidden under all those clothes."

Rachel didn't understand his English so he used his hand to mimic holding a gun. After he inspected her, he waved her forward.

"You're finished. Move along."

Rachel waited for her mother and Hensche and the three of them went into the tent. They were met with men in yellow overalls, wearing huge masks. Rachel recognized the smell of DDT, the chemical used to get rid of lice and bugs, from the DP camps. When it was her turn to be sprayed, she gritted her teeth and closed her eyes, trying not to breathe. The DDT smelled awful and left gray dust on her skin and

British soldiers helped those who had been wounded in the battle reach the waiting ambulances. The passengers were silent as the coffin holding their beloved second officer, Bill Bernstein, was carried off the ship.

hair. The inspection was over and they waited on the dock.

There were three transport ships tied up at the pier: the *Runnymede Park*, the *Empire Rival*, and the *Ocean Vigour*. The soldiers were separating the refugees into three groups. Rachel and her family were assigned to board the *Ocean Vigour*. Rachel looked at the ship in horror. Half the deck was covered with a barbed wire cage. It looked like a prison.

"This is a hospital ship," said the soldier who gave them their instructions. "It has milk and food for mothers and children. You will be very comfortable until you get to Cyprus. It will only take a few hours to get there."

Rachel looked for Miriam. She saw her in a line leading to the *Empire Rival*. She started to run over to her, but the soldier blocked her path.

"Sorry, Miss. You have to stay here."

"No English," Rachel said, using the words she had learned on the ship.

The soldier indicated that she should remain in her own line.

Rachel pointed to Miriam who was trying to leave her line and come to Rachel.

Miriam broke away and ran over to her. "I want to stay with you."

Rachel gave the soldier a pleading look.

Mama stepped forward and took Miriam's arm. She glared at the soldier.

He relented. "All right, Ma'am." He waved them forward. "Now all of you, move along."

Rachel and Miriam linked arms. "Thank you," Miriam whispered as they mounted the gangplank. "Thank you for making me part of your family."

As they boarded the ship, Aviva came up to them. "Are you all right?"

"Yes," replied Rachel. "Are you coming on our ship?"

"No." Aviva pointed. "I'm on the *Runnymede Park*. But I'll be with you in Cyprus." She gave them each a hug. "Get some sleep. I'll see you when we arrive in Cyprus."

CHAPTER 18
Aboard the Ocean Vigour

July 19, 1947

"Can you believe this? We are in a prison." Hensche looked around in disgust.

The *Exodus* passengers were herded into the part of the deck that was surrounded by a cage of steel netting topped with coils of rusty barbed wire. When they descended to the hold, conditions were even worse. It was midsummer and the air was thick and hot in the closed space. There were no bunks. Everyone was given a brown blanket and told to use it to sleep on the floor. The space was so crowded that finding a place to sit, let alone sleep, was almost impossible. Hensche pointed to an empty spot against the wall. "Let's take off some of these clothes."

They stripped off layer after layer and folded everything in a neat pile.

"I feel like a sardine in a can," Rachel said as she squeezed in between her mother and sister.

"It's not for long," Hensche soothed her. "Let's try to sleep. In the morning, we'll be in Cyprus."

Yes, we'll be in Cyprus, Rachel thought as she closed her eyes. *Not Eretz Yisroel.*

In the morning the air in the hold was so hot it was unbreathable. The mood had turned ugly. The ship should have arrived at Cyprus hours earlier. *Where are we?* The question reverberated through the crowd.

"Why are we being herded like cattle? We are prisoners, just like we were with the Nazis."

A short man with dark hair slicked back off his forehead stood up. He raised his voice. Rachel recognized Mordecai Rosman, the partisan hero Saul had pointed out to her earlier. She was surprised that such a strong voice could come from such a small, wiry body. "Everyone, listen to me. The British think they have beaten us but we are not beaten. We are not slaves. Whatever happens we must continue our struggle. They can't keep us in a closed compartment without even the barest of necessities such as fresh air."

"Get them to open the hatch," someone shouted.

Angry voices joined in. A group of young men stormed up the stairs and pounded on the hatch. "Open up! Open this hatch. We need air."

Finally, after much pounding and shouting, the hatch opened. Rachel strained to hear what they were saying, but a wailing siren drowned out their voices. After a few minutes, the siren stopped and a boy's head popped through the open hatch. Rachel was delighted to see that it was Saul.

"It's all right now," he exulted. "They'll keep the hatch open and you can come up on deck."

"How did you convince the soldiers to let us come up?" Rachel looked at Saul in awe.

"It wasn't me. It was Mordecai Rosman." He convinced them that with the hatch closed and no air, they would have a lot of sick people on their hands."

Rachel look at Rosman, who was talking to a group of people, gesturing with his hands as if telling a story. His expression was animated and the people around him listened in silence.

"He's quite a leader." Saul gave him an appreciative look. "I'm glad he's on our side."

"Where is David?" Rachel looked around the crowded deck. "Is he all right?"

"He's on one of the other ships." Saul made a sour face. "I found him on the dock in Haifa. He was on a stretcher. They smashed his arm. It's in a sling. He has some bad bruises, but he is healing. We tried to stay together but they even broke up families."

Rachel looked out at the ocean. "Where do you think we're going? They said we're going to Cyprus."

"If we were going to Cyprus, we'd already be there. We're going west and that means Europe. Look." Saul pointed to the sky.

Rachel shaded her eyes and looked up at the bright ball of sun halfway up the sky. She turned and saw the other two ships behind them. All three ships were surrounded by British destroyers.

"At least you have your mother and sister in this prison of a ship," Miriam said in a sad voice. "Promise me, Rachel, that whatever happens, we'll stay together."

"I promise." Rachel took her hand. "We're cousins now."

"And I'll be your brother," Saul quipped. His lips were still swollen and his eye was a sickly shade of yellow. For a moment, his face darkened and his eyes clouded over. Then he shook his head and smiled. "We can help each other when we get where we are going."

Rachel looked at the sun. "Wherever that is."

PART TWO

Return to Europe

CHAPTER 19
Port-de-Bouc, France

August 2, 1947

Day after day, the ships sailed without sighting land. People were angry and restless. The optimism that had strengthened them on the *Exodus* was fading as fast as the onboard conditions were deteriorating. There were only two latrines for 1,500 people. The hot meals they had been fed on *Exodus* were just a memory. Now they ate British rations, mostly tea and hard biscuits. Rachel and her friends passed the time by playing games, telling stories, and listening to the angry conversations swirling around them.

"Where are they taking us?"

"If they were taking us back to France, we would be there by now."

"We want to return to Palestine."

In the evenings, passengers organized singing and storytelling. On Friday nights they held Shabbat services in the hold. Still, time passed slowly.

Then one morning, two weeks after leaving Haifa, the ship slowed down. They could see land. Rachel stood at the rail with Saul and Miriam. "Look!" She pointed to a small motorboat buzzing along beside them.

A man was standing up and waving at them. He cupped his hands around his mouth and called out in French, "Don't get off the ship! We are with you. The whole world is with you. Stay strong!"

Miriam stared in amazement. Could this be true? Did the world even know they existed, let alone care?

"Look – more boats!" Rachel pointed excitedly.

And sure enough, there were small boats sailing near each of the three ships with people shouting to the refugees in French, Yiddish, and Hebrew to keep up their spirits. "How do they know about us?" Rachel asked. "How do they know who we are?"

"They must have heard the Voice of Israel radio broadcast," said Saul. "And there were dozens of reporters on the dock at Haifa. The soldiers wouldn't let them near us. They were kept behind a barrier. But I saw them with cameras. Maybe they told our story to the world. One of them, her name is Ruth Gruber, has been writing about us every day and sending her stories to newspapers in America."

Rachel was puzzled. "How do you know that reporter's name? We haven't seen any newspapers."

"One of the refugees who speaks English told me he overheard a British soldier say that the Gruber woman is a real pest because she keeps writing stories that are stirring up trouble for them."

"Then I like her." Rachel looked at the boats that were now approaching the *Runnymede Park*. Maybe the world would come to their aid after all. "If people know what the British are doing, they will help us."

"Maybe," Saul said. "Or maybe they will once again turn against us."

"Saul Cohen, you are such a pessimist. Why can't you believe that some people are good?"

Saul's eyes narrowed. "Because I've seen the worst that human beings can do."

The motorboat was coming back toward the *Ocean Vigour*. A man in a light gray suit and straw hat stood up and waved. "Be brave! We are on your side."

"See," Rachel said. "We do have friends." She waved back at the man.

The *Ocean Vigour* and the other two ships dropped anchor just off-shore. So far, no one had told the passengers where they were.

"Can you read that sign?" Rachel pointed to the dock.

Miriam shaded her eyes with her hand. "Port-de-Bouc. We're in France again."

Saul turned to Miriam. "You're from France. Aren't you glad to be back?" he asked sarcastically.

"It is not my home anymore," Miriam said.

"Why do you say that?" Rachel questioned her. "You were saved by a French family."

"Yes. The Gerards were wonderful. Others were not so good. There were people in the village who would have turned me over to the Nazis if they had known who I really was."

"At least we're not in Germany," Rachel said trying to make her feel better.

Saul changed the subject. "I heard that at one time the British wanted to send us to Uganda."

"Uganda? Where is that?"

"It's a country in Africa." He leaned over and thumped his thighs as if they were drums. "Africa! We'd live with lions and elephants."

"And giraffes," Miriam giggled.

"See, I made you laugh." Saul gave her a warm smile.

"So we're in France," Rachel said, in a resigned voice. "We're still not in Palestine."

"Being in France has its advantages." Rachel took a bite of a peach and sighed with pleasure as the juice dribbled down her chin. In the two days since they had arrived in Port-de-Bouc, boats loaded with fresh food and other supplies were keeping the passengers well fed and in relatively good spirits. It was a welcome change after the hard biscuits and tea they had been surviving on for two long weeks. Rachel and her friends watched as the British sailors inspected every package. They pierced the cans with bayonets and removed newspapers and anything else they didn't want the passengers to have. Then they passed the food through the wire cage.

"I had forgotten what fresh bread tastes like," Miriam said as she bit into a soft roll.

After being at sea for seventeen days before docking in Port-de-Bouc, conditions had become so bad that everyone on board was worried about diseases such as typhus and measles breaking out. So this stop was a welcome respite, especially when the local residents began supplying them with healthy food, books, and games for the children.

Rachel and Miriam sat on the deck with Saul.

"I heard that the reason we were at sea for so long was because the British wanted to bring us back to France but the French government refused to let the ships dock. So we had to keep sailing around until the French finally gave in. No country wants us. Meanwhile newspapers all over the world are writing about us," Miriam told Rachel.

"Where did you hear all that?"

She smiled. "News gets smuggled on board with the food and then it spreads."

"Like the measles?"

"I hope they don't inoculate us against the news like they did against the measles."

A few passengers had caught measles, so everyone on board was given a shot. Rachel shuddered at the memory. "Well, they can't immunize us against the news. The world is cheering for us."

As they sat inside their cage, gorging on fresh food, the girls allowed themselves a moment of hope. Perhaps, with the world watching, the British would relent.

CHAPTER 20

World Support for a Ship Going Nowhere

Once people realized that the stay in Port-du-Bouc would be lengthy, they organized a schedule for the children. In the morning their task was to help prepare and distribute food. In the afternoon they had classes in Hebrew and other subjects. Every day small boats continued to bring food, books, games, and writing materials for the children. And with each delivery, the soldiers continued to inspect everything.

"Do they really think there are bombs inside the canned sardines?" Rachel asked as she and Saul waited at the cage fence to get their food.

"You can make a bomb out of any container," Saul said with assurance.

Rachel looked at him with respect. "Could you make a bomb with this can?"

"If I had the right materials," he said. He gave her a sly smile. "Do you want me to show you?"

"No!" Then she laughed. "You're joking. Aren't you?"

A soldier unlocked the gate and as it creaked open Rachel and Saul went out to collect their rations.

"It's strange being on the outside," Rachel said, turning to look back through the wire cage.

"Hurry it up. There are others waiting behind you," the soldier giving out the food scolded.

They selected what they needed from the boxes of canned goods and fresh food. Rachel filled her sack with bread, two cans of kosher corned beef, tomatoes, a cucumber and a jar of apricot jam. "Look," she pointed to the Hebrew writing on the label. "It's from Palestine."

They walked back through the gate to the port side of the ship where Hensche, Rachel's mother, and Miriam were waiting for them. "*B'tai avon,*" Rachel said, using the Hebrew words for good appetite as they settled down to enjoy their meal, the highlight of their day.

In spite of the food and books, life on board the *Ocean Vigour* had become nearly unbearable. The August heat was blistering. Inside their cage, the passengers sweltered under the broiling sun in temperatures of 104°F (40°C) – what they heard was the hottest summer in the region's history. Rachel and Miriam spent most of their time reading and talking on deck, trying to keep cool.

They were sitting on deck one day when two men wearing the white coats of doctors sat beside them. One had dark curly hair. The other was blond and blue-eyed.

"*Shalom*," the dark-haired man said in Hebrew. "My name is Avram." He pointed to the blond man. "He is Lev. We are both from Palestine."

"From Palestine?" Rachel's heart was pounding. "Are you with the Haganah?"

"Yes," said Avram. "We dressed as doctors so we could get on board. But now we will stay with you for the rest of your time on this ship."

"Do you know Aviva?" Rachel whispered.

"Of course. She was with you on the *Exodus*. Now she is on the *Runnymede Park*." Avram reached into his pocket and handed each of the girls a coin. "This is money from Palestine. Keep it and spend it once you are there."

Rachel cradled the coin in the palm of her hand. "Thank you. Please tell us, do people really want to know about us? Are they writing about us in the newspapers?"

"You'd be surprised," said Avram. "The refugees on these three ships are famous. The whole town of Port-de-Bouc is filled with reporters, British and French government officials, people that work to help refugees, and Haganah members, like us. They meet in cafés on the wharf and send out news about what is happening to you. There's one American woman reporter who is trying to get on board. She's on our side. I've spoken with her."

Lev added, "She has been following your story. Now she has come to Port-de-Bouc to write about you."

"Is that Ruth Gruber? We've heard about her. What has she been writing about us?" Miriam asked.

"She has been telling the whole world that you are brave people who should be allowed to live in your own country," said Avram.

"I wish I could meet her," Rachel said.

"Maybe you'll get the chance. She keeps asking the British authorities to let her come aboard. She's pretty determined. I bet she'll get her way."

"That makes us feel better," Miriam said.

"Thank you for talking to us and for the coin." Rachel fingered the silver coin.

Avram stood up. "We have to go now. Remember, that coin is to spend in Palestine."

CHAPTER 21

An Offer from the French Government

They had been in France for a week and everyone was getting restless wondering what would happen next. Rumors were as thick as the swarms of mosquitoes that formed after dark each night.

"I heard that a delegation from the French government is coming on board." Saul told them in a knowing voice.

"Where did you hear that?"

"Oh, around."

"Around where?" Rachel asked.

Reluctantly, Saul answered. "One of the crewmembers trades information for chocolate. You can't tell anyone else. If he gets into trouble, we won't get more information."

"What else has he told you?"

"That the French have finally spoken up on our behalf," Saul continued.

"Do you think they've convinced the British to take us back to Palestine?" Rachel asked hopefully.

Miriam gave her a sympathetic look. "If only you were right."

Saul stood and stretched. "Well if they are coming aboard, they must have something to say. I'm going to see what else I can find out." He gave them a mock salute and walked away.

After lunch Saul was back. "I told you!" he said. "Here they come. Look!" He pointed to the dock as the French delegation members briskly mounted the gangplank. Everyone gathered on the deck to hear what they had to say.

One man stepped forward. Rachel had never seen him before. He was of medium height with a kindly face and thinning, gray hair. In spite of the heat, he was dressed in a dark suit, a crisp white shirt, and a blue-and-white striped tie. He introduced himself as a Jewish leader and a representative of the French government. He unfolded a piece of paper and read an announcement to the refugees, first in French and then in Yiddish and Hebrew. It offered immediate French citizenship to any refugee who would voluntarily leave the ship. "France is willing to accept all 4,500 *Exodus* passengers into our country!" he

Mordecai Rosman

Mordecai Rosman was born in Poland. He joined a youth movement that trained young people to go to Palestine. During the war, he worked with the Jewish Underground to help Jews escape from the Nazis. He saved many Jewish lives by leading people to safety in the woods after the Warsaw Ghetto Uprising.

He always dreamed of living in Palestine. After the war, when the opportunity arose, he boarded the *Exodus* as an illegal immigrant. On board the ship, he became a leader amongst his fellow refugees and spoke on their behalf in powerful and emotional speeches.

said, spreading his arms wide, as if in welcome.

The passengers looked at each other. France was now prepared to accept the refugees. Would anyone take the offer?

Then out of the crowd, Mordecai Rosman stepped forward. After confronting the British on the *Exodus* he had become the natural leader of the refugees.

"On behalf of my fellow passengers, I wish to thank the French government for its generous offer to receive us as French citizens." He paused. "However, we are forced to reject the offer, because there is just one place in the world where we want to live. That is our homeland, Eretz Yisroel. There, and only there, will we leave these ships of our own free will!"

Everyone applauded and shouted their approval. Mordecai Rosman turned to the group and continued. "Everyone has the right to decide for himself or herself. If someone wants to get off, they can do so. No one will interfere with you." He stopped speaking and waited. Nobody said a word. After a lengthy pause, he addressed the French official. "I am telling you, no one is leaving this ship." Turning to the British officers he pleaded, "Take us to Haifa and let us disembark there."

The French officials seemed puzzled that the passengers were rejecting their generous offer. The British were furious. Rachel looked at the officer standing next to the French official. His face was the color of a ripe tomato.

The officials left to deliver their message to the other two ships.

"Do you think anyone on the other two ships will accept their offer?" Rachel asked Saul.

"I doubt it." He shook his head. "The British are stubborn, but we are more stubborn."

"Saul, tell me about Mr. Rosman. Did you know him when you were with the partisans?"

"I wish I had." Saul looked to where the man was talking to a group of people. "We all knew about him. He was a legend. He was a hero in the Warsaw Ghetto where he saved many lives."

Rachel looked at the man with new respect. "I heard that conditions in the Warsaw Ghetto were even worse than in the Budapest Ghetto."

"Very few people survived the Warsaw Ghetto," Saul said grimly. "Those who didn't die of starvation or disease were sent to Treblinka,

Majdanek, and other death camps. And when the Nazis destroyed the ghetto, Mordecai Rosman escaped to the forest and fought against the Nazis for the rest of the war."

CHAPTER 22

Another Standoff

The offer from France was delivered to all three ships, but only two pregnant women who were ready to give birth and two men who were gravely ill got off. The rest of the people remained, enduring the heat and the overcrowding. And, as they had on the *Exodus*, they made the best of their time on board.

"I wish they would turn off that light." Rachel put her arm over her eyes, trying to block out the glare. Sleep was impossible because a giant searchlight on the deck was kept on all night and the huge floodlights in the hold were never turned off. In addition, there was the clattering of soldiers' boots pacing up and down on the grillwork that covered the hold. Sleep came late and morning came early. By 6 a.m. everyone on board was wide awake.

"Ouch!" Rachel squirmed on the floor of the hold.

"Sit still," commanded Hensche. "I have to get these knots out of your hair."

"Does it have to hurt so much?"

"Do you want to get lice?"

Rachel shuddered. Lice were a problem in cramped and dirty spaces. They carried a disease called typhus. With the ship so over-crowded, people could easily become sick. Rachel, Hensche, and their mother washed their hands and faces with seawater that was hauled up in buckets. And every morning Hensche combed Rachel's long, brown hair and twisted it into two thick braids.

After their morning chores and afternoon classes the children played on deck if the weather was good. The adults talked about politics and shared whatever information had filtered into the ship.

At night, the women took turns washing clothes. There was a basin of salt water in front of each latrine on deck. They used these to scrub dresses and shorts and shirts, which were becoming more ragged with each wash, then hung them on the barbed wire fence to dry.

The British kept urging everyone to go ashore. When the Haganah people translated and broadcast the British messages, they added *lo mit an alef,* a Yiddish expression meaning "emphatically No." People called from one ship to another: "Don't listen to them. Stay on board.

Don't go ashore." Every time they did this, the British soldiers blasted the ship's horn to drown out their voices.

After days of unbearable heat, it started to rain. But this was no ordinary rain – torrential storms forced everyone down into the hold. Now, even during daytime hours, there were 1,500 bodies crammed into the small space. Water streamed through the grills above their heads. Thunder rumbled across the sky, and the ship shook with the force of the storm. For four days and nights, the passengers endured these awful conditions. When their leaders asked the British to give them a tarpaulin for cover on deck, the guards answered that they were free to go ashore any time.

CHAPTER 23
Hunger Strike

"They've taken our books!" Sarah, the children's French teacher was on the verge of tears. "The British have confiscated all our reading materials, even our Bibles."

"They can do whatever they want because they are in control," Mordecai Rosman growled. He waved his arms and people from all over the deck gathered around him. "They have not only taken our books, they have burned them! There is only one way left for us to confront them," he shouted. "We will declare a hunger strike to show them they cannot control us. The world will know what is going on here!"

People stared at him in stunned silence. Burning books? Children's books? The Bible? Yet a hunger strike was a desperate measure.

Especially now, when there was such wonderful food from French and American friends.

"Why do you think a hunger strike will work?" one woman demanded.

"It will show the British that they can't force us to do what they want. We control our own fate."

"No one is compelled to fast," he emphasized. "But those of you who believe, as I do, that we have the right to be treated as free and equal human beings will join me in beating the British. By refusing food we are exerting our rights as independent thinkers. The publicity about a hunger strike will make us look good and the British look bad." He paused. "We have become news. The world is watching what happens here. Anything we can do to win sympathy will help us and hurt the British."

"It will be like fasting on Yom Kippur," shouted a young man.

"We were forced to go hungry in the camps and ghettos," said a woman by his side. "This time we will do it by choice."

"That's the spirit!" Mordecai stamped his foot. "Pregnant women, small children, and anyone who is sick must not strike. From now on we will send back the launches filled with food."

"Even the chocolate?" moaned Miriam.

"We'll eat lots of chocolate in Palestine," Rachel teased her.

"So, do we strike?" yelled Mordecai.

"Yes!" everyone shouted.

The hunger strike was on.

Time passed very slowly. "This isn't the first time I've gone without food." Mama closed her eyes as if calling up memories. "Stay where you are and don't talk so much. Talking takes energy," she told the girls.

"How long do you think this strike will last?" Miriam asked.

"I guess it depends on what the British decide to do."

"Can you believe that the British have announced to the world that there is no hunger strike aboard the refugee ships?" Saul said, his voice filled with disgust.

Rachel looked at him in confusion. Her stomach was growling and she was trying not to think of all the delicious food going to waste. "How do you know that?"

"I promised my source chocolate when the strike is over. They can't believe it either. They've seen the launches return to shore full of the food we refuse to eat." He moved to the side of the cage and looked out at the water.

Rachel followed his gaze as motor launches carrying French police approached the ship.

"Uh oh! What do you suppose they want now?"

Passengers around them shouted: "We will not come down. We will come down only in Palestine."

"Look at that." Rachel pointed to the top of the cage where people had strung up signs in English and French. "Miriam, you read French. What do they say?"

"They say, 'Open the doors of Palestine, our only hope.'"

"I wonder how long the French will allow us to stay. We've been here for three weeks. What do you think, Saul?"

"The French have said they won't force us to leave. So now it's up to the British to decide what to do with us."

It wasn't long before they had the decision.

CHAPTER 24
Hard Decisions

August 21, 1947

The hunger strike had its effect. Just 24 hours into the strike, shortly after noon the next day, British and French officials came on board the ship. British soldiers distributed leaflets. The message was also written on the ship's blackboard in German, Yiddish, and Polish. A British official read it aloud:

> *To the passengers on the* Runnymede Park, Empire Rival, Ocean Vigour. *This announcement is made to you on behalf of the British Government. Those of you who do not begin to disembark at Port-de-Bouc before six p.m. tomorrow, August 22nd, will be taken by sea to Hamburg.*

Everyone stood in shocked silence. Mordecai Rosman spoke up. "We need time to discuss this new situation."

The man who had read the notice nodded. "You have half an hour." He and his group stepped out of the cage. When they were out of earshot, everyone gathered around Mr. Rosman.

"How can they send us to Germany?" shouted a man. "To the country that tried to wipe us all off the face of the earth!"

"Do you want to get off this ship?" Mr. Rosman countered.

"No!" a chorus of shouts drowned him out.

"We will only get off in Eretz Yisroel," said Saul.

A woman held up her baby. "I want my baby to live in our own country."

"This is a big decision," Mordecai Rosman said gravely. "I want everyone to think carefully and then we will take a vote."

❀ ❀ ❀

Rachel looked at her mother and sister. "What are we going to do?"

Their mother looked uncertain. "Do we want to go back to Germany to another DP camp when we can stay in France and start new lives?"

"Mama," Rachel assumed her most adult voice, "do you think that France will be any different? We will still be Jews in someone else's country."

"She's right." Hensche gave her sister an approving look. "We've come this far. We should stay on this ship."

Their mother looked at her younger daughter. Rachel could almost see the thoughts passing across her mother's face. Mama was tired. She wanted to stop running. It was what they all wanted. But to get off the ship now would be a defeat. Rachel held her breath.

"Very well then," her mother said in a solemn voice. "We will stay on the ship."

"Thank you." Rachel hugged her mother around the waist. "Thank you, Mama."

"So, do we stay or go?" Mordecai Rosman asked when everyone gathered around him again.

"STAY!"

"We will vote. All those who want to remain on board?"

A sea of hands waved in the air.

When the officials were within earshot again, he called out: "We have voted. Our decision is that we stay on the ship."

Votes were taken on the other two ships with the same result. The *Exodus* passengers would not give in to British demands.

Once again, the *Ocean Vigour* was draped in darkness. The passengers were unusually quiet after their decision to stay aboard. Like most of the others, Rachel was on deck with her mother and Hensche. The hunger strike was over, but the food she had eaten now sat in her stomach like a rock. They had made their decision to stay on board, even if it meant going back to Germany. At least it was no longer ruled by the Nazis. Allied troops from America, Britain, and Russia had won the war and were now in charge. But the refugees still remembered Germany as the country that had launched the Nazis' plan to kill every Jew in Europe.

"Mama, listen." Rachel jumped to her feet and pointed at two boats filled with people standing and again shouting through loud-speakers: "You are not alone. People from all over the world have heard about you and support your fight."

"I've heard that we are receiving food from America and Canada, as well as France and other countries," said Hensche. "Many organizations are raising money for the supplies."

Her mother smiled. "I believe we have touched people's hearts."

The ship's horn blasted and drowned out the voices from the boats. But the message had been received.

Rachel turned to her mother. "Do you think all these people will really fight for us?" she asked.

"Yes, I think they will." Her mother pulled her close. "And with their help, we might yet get to our homeland."

❀ ❀ ❀

Rachel went in search of Avram. She found him with a group of young adults. When he saw Rachel, he motioned for her to join them. Rachel shook her head. "I want to talk to you," she mouthed.

"Are you all right?" Avram's dark eyes were narrowed in concern.

"Yes." Rachel chewed her lip. "I have a question."

"I'll answer if I can." Avram steered her to a quiet corner. "What is it?"

"Why are the British taking us to Germany and not to England?"

"A good question. Here, sit."

They moved to a corner of the deck, under the bridge. Rachel sat and leaned back against the bulkhead.

"After winning the war, the British, the Americans, and the Russians divided Germany into three parts. Hamburg is in the section of Germany that is controlled by the British. That is why they are able to take us there. And why are they not taking us to England? The answer is that they don't want more Jewish refugees."

"That is why we will keep fighting to get you – and every Jew who wants to come – to Eretz Yisroel." Avram pointed to the sky. "Look at the stars. So many. It is such a big universe and all we are asking for is a tiny piece of land where we feel safe and secure."

CHAPTER 25

Meeting the Press in Marseilles

Still in France, the ship sailed to the port of Marseilles. As the *Ocean Vigour* pulled up to the dock, it was greeted by the hooting of ships' horns.

Miriam rushed up to Rachel. "Every ship in the port is saluting *us*."

They peered in awe through the wire cage. All over the harbor boats and ships were blasting their horns, while sailors lined their decks and cheered the passengers. On shore people filled the street and leaned out of windows, waving and blowing kisses.

"Stay strong!" they shouted. "We know your plight. We are with you."

"Look!" Rachel pointed excitedly as her mother and Hensche joined them. "Can you believe it? This cheering is for us."

Now all the passengers were on deck, laughing, crying, and calling to the people on shore. Rachel jumped up and down, waving both arms and people waved back and shouted greetings. Their voices were music, a beautiful symphony that raised everyone's spirits. Meanwhile the ship's crew carried supplies onboard preparing for the voyage to Germany.

A first the British didn't allow reporters onto the ships. But on the last day the ship was in port they lifted the ban. The passengers heard that one of the journalists allowed to board the *Ocean Vigour* was Ruth Gruber.

"What has she been reporting? What does she say about the British?" Rachel pressed Avram for details. Since newspapers were banned, passengers had to rely on people who had been ashore to tell them what was happening.

"She says that they should let you go to Palestine. She was in Haifa and saw the terrible damage to the *Exodus* and how badly you were treated. She is telling the world the truth about you."

"Does she say what happened to Captain Ike?"

Avram smiled. "When we docked in Haifa he went back to his home. So did Yossi Harel. But I'm sure they are both following your story and rooting for you."

That afternoon, Rachel and Miriam, along with other refugees, waited anxiously for the reporter to appear.

"Look, there she is," Miriam pointed excitedly as a group appeared on the deck. Ruth Gruber was a petite woman with short dark hair. She had a leather camera bag slung over her shoulder. She, another reporter, and two men in dark suits who looked like government officials climbed up to the bridge where the captain greeted them. Ruth Gruber looked down at the cage where hundreds of refugees were staring up at her. She pulled out her camera and snapped a picture.

The male reporter looked down at the crowd gathered in the cage. He cupped his hands and shouted. "Do you want to get off this ship?"

"No!" came the answer.

Then Mordecai Rosman called up to them. "We will disembark willingly in Palestine."

The reporters came down to the deck and walked to the cage. "Please let us in!" Ruth Gruber insisted. The guard hesitated until the captain motioned for him to obey. He unbolted the gate and the reporters stepped inside to speak to the people. The refugees crowded around Ruth Gruber. She followed the crowd down a slippery flight of stairs into the hold. Staring in horror at their living conditions, she stopped in front of a young woman who was nursing her baby. "Why are you doing this? You could be safe on shore in France."

"I am doing this for her," the woman replied, holding out the child. "I want my daughter to grow up in a free country where no one will put her in a concentration camp and where she can be proud to be a Jew."

Another woman held up her child to be photographed. He was about two years old and looked directly at Ruth Gruber with his clear blue eyes. When she reached for his hand, he clutched her thumb. "He is beautiful and he deserves a home," she said as she took his picture.

A man with gray hair and stooped shoulders handed her a scrap

Ruth Gruber

Born in Brooklyn, New York in 1911, Ruth was 19 when she won a scholarship to study in Germany and saw the anti-Semitism that was rising there. When she returned home, she became a journalist and later a war correspondent. In 1941, in the midst of the war, she conducted a secret mission for President Franklin Roosevelt when she brought 1,000 Jewish refugees from Naples, Italy to the United States. For that mission, she was given the honorary rank of general. As a general, if she had been caught by the Nazis, she would have to be housed and fed as a prisoner of war. Without that rank she would be shot as a spy.

After the war, Ruth worked as a foreign correspondent for the *New York Herald Tribune*. That job took her to Palestine, where she heard the radio broadcast from the *Exodus*. She contacted her paper for permission to cover the refugees' story, which she followed from beginning to end. She wanted to tell the world what was *really* happening to the *Exodus* and its passengers.

of paper. "My sister lives in New York. Please write and tell her that I'm alive."

Others echoed his request.

"My uncle is in Haifa. Let him know that I am on my way."

"I have cousins on Cyprus. They thought I'd be there. Tell them I'm safe and that we will meet in Eretz Yisroel."

Ruth Gruber listened to all the pleas. "I will send your messages."

Then Mordecai Rosman spoke again.

"Forget the messages. This is what you should write. Write that thirty-five years after the British government issued the Balfour Declaration promising us a homeland, we are being sent back to Germany. The British want to stop what they call illegal immigration. But we Jews are afraid of nothing. Tell them that we will not surrender!"

That evening, Ruth Gruber stood on the quay. As she watched the three prison ships move out to sea, surrounded by British destroyers, she marveled at the courage and determination of the people on board. *They are people such as the world has never seen,* she wrote in her notes. *They are the bravest people I have ever known.*

CHAPTER 26
The Trip to Nowhere

Once again the *Exodus* passengers were afloat on the Mediterranean Sea. Only this time, they were sailing west toward Germany, not east toward Palestine. In spite of the awful conditions on board and the horror of being sent back to Germany, only seven people had stayed behind in France.

Once at sea, Rachel felt the mood on board changing. They had been on the prison ships for almost six weeks. Until now, they had kept alive a sliver of hope that the British would relent and let them go to Palestine, the only country where they would live voluntarily. With their departure from Marseilles, that hope had vanished like a puff of smoke in the wind.

Out on the ocean, the water became choppy and the ship rocked back and forth.

"Oh," Miriam put her head in her hands. "I can't remember what it's like to stand on dry land."

"Try to forget that we're on the water." Rachel took a deep breath. She was determined not to become seasick.

"I miss the food in France," Miriam said as she cracked open a moldy biscuit.

"You mean you don't like porridge with worms in it?" Rachel's eyes sparkled with mischief.

"Think of it as extra protein," Avram joined in. After coming on board as a doctor, he had changed into khaki shorts and shirt so he would look like a passenger. "In the old days, on our kibbutz we didn't have much meat. But we had lots of olives. Olives are a good source of protein," he said. "So we ate them for breakfast and lunch and dinner."

"I've never eaten olives," Rachel said.

"You'll grow to like them." Avram laughed. "And oranges, this big." He made a circle with his hands.

"Tell us more about the kibbutz."

"It is beautiful." Avram's face had a faraway look. "In Poland, we lived in a village where life was hard for Jews. The peasants accused us of poisoning the water in the wells. Can you imagine that?" He shook his head. "They beat us up. That is how I learned to fight." He held up his fists. "My father said that for a Jew the only place to live was Eretz Yisroel. We joined a group that was learning to farm so we could work when we got there."

"When did you leave Poland?" Rachel asked.

"In 1935. Our whole group – there were about twenty of us – went to Italy and sailed from Genoa. When we got to Palestine, we were sent to the Galilee in the north of Palestine."

"How old were you when you left Poland?"

"I was twelve. But my sister Sarah, who was born a year after we arrived, is a Sabra," he said in a proud voice. "Our kibbutz was started in 1932. The first people to settle were pioneers. They had to clear swamps. It was not all cleared when we arrived and we had to fight mosquitoes so big we thought they were birds." He laughed. "Some people got sick from malaria and other diseases. But we worked hard and turned the swamp into a garden. Today we grow cucumbers and tomatoes and grapefruit." He smiled. "You will come for a visit."

"If we ever get there." Rachel sighed. Then she brightened. "I mean *when* we get there."

"That's the spirit." Avram slapped her on the back. "Now you sound like a Sabra."

❀ ❀ ❀

When it started to rain, Rachel went into the hold and squeezed into the space beside her mother and Hensche. Exhausted from the tension of the day, she soon fell asleep. When she went on deck the next morning, she saw seagulls circling overhead, a sure sign that they were approaching land.

The water was calmer. The air was warm, but not as hot as it had been in Marseilles. That afternoon the ship anchored in the British naval base at the Straits of Gibraltar. Gibraltar was a craggy, rocky mountain, so different from the gentle hills of Haifa. They stayed in Gibraltar for two days while the ships took on fuel and supplies. On the third day, August 29, 1947, the three ships once again set sail. The passengers could no longer deny that they were on their way north, the final stretch of the voyage to Hamburg.

From Gibraltar they sailed into the North Atlantic Ocean, through the English Channel, and then into the North Sea, where the rough water made many people seasick again. As conditions worsened, tempers flared. Fights broke out over space in the crowded hold. Rachel and Miriam spent as much time as they could on deck to escape the smell of sickness and bad air in the hold. And then there was the food. They were back on British rations.

"I don't miss France but I do miss the fresh bread and fruit." Miriam looked ruefully at the package of dry biscuits that was her breakfast.

"You'd better eat it," Hensche said. She placed an arm around Miriam's shoulder. "It's all the food you'll get until supper."

"Yum." Rachel licked her lips. "I can hardly wait for the potato water that they call soup."

"Do you like it with or without maggots?" Miriam giggled.

"With, of course," Rachel mugged. "We need our protein."

"You girls are good sports." Hensche smiled at them. "I know this is hard, but you are making the best of it."

Hensche watched them move across the deck to their Hebrew class. *Such brave girls*, she thought. She was proud of her sister. Throughout this whole ordeal Rachel had been strong. Hensche thought back to their time in Budapest when Rachel often got into trouble because of her high spirits and independent nature. Even in the ghetto, Rachel had been a bright spirit, cheering them with her antics. Hensche sighed. *Rachel deserves a home.* She looked around the crowded deck. *We all do.*

PART THREE
Detour to Germany

The Desert News, September 8, 1947

CHAPTER 27
On the Elbe River

September 7, 1947

Something about the ship felt different to Rachel. It wasn't rocking. They were sailing on water as smooth as glass. Trees and houses lined the shores on both sides of the ship.

"Where are we?" Rachel asked Avram.

"On the Elbe River. We are almost in Hamburg."

Rachel turned to Hensche. "I never thought we'd be back here in Germany," her sister said in a tired voice.

"It is only temporary," Rachel insisted. "We *will* get to Palestine."

"How can you still believe that? You are such an optimist, Rachel. Nothing frightens you."

You are wrong, Hensche. I do get frightened. During the war, I was terrified of the Nazi soldiers. And I was scared when our building burned down. In the ghetto, when we cowered in the cellars during bombing raids, I had nightmares. But then the war ended. Russian soldiers liberated us. That's when I stopped being afraid.

People came up from below to gaze at the shore. Many were angry and protesting.

"We'll do what we did in France. We'll refuse to leave the ship."

"This isn't France. It's Germany."

"It's the British occupied zone in Germany. The British military is in command here."

Others thought it was time to cooperate. They didn't want more violence.

"We have no choice." Rachel's mother came up to them. "Girls, we will do this peacefully. Please."

Rachel stood at the rail in the fog as the ship docked.

"Well, here we are," her mother said through clenched teeth. Her arms were folded across her chest. "Back in Germany, where we began."

The morning dawned bright and clear. Soon the fog burned off and Rachel could see the dock. It was filled with British soldiers wearing steel helmets. *To protect themselves from us,* thought Rachel.

*Rows of British soldiers stood guard
as the refugees were removed from
the train in Hamburg, Germany.*

She could also see doctors, nurses, and ambulance trucks. She was standing with her mother and Hensche. They had all their belongings with them in preparation for leaving the ship.

Rachel saw Miriam and motioned for her to join them. "Whatever happens, stay with us."

"Thank you." Miriam gave her a grateful smile.

They waited together in silence until it was their turn. As they walked down the gangplank, Rachel studied the faces of the other refugees leaving the ship. They walked listlessly, dragging their feet. No one spoke.

"What's that?" Rachel asked as a burst of noise erupted. People were screaming. There were loud thuds. Rachel watched in horror as troops stormed up the gangplank of the third ship, the *Runnymede Park* and then returned, dragging people and pulling them onto the dock.

A group of reporters pressed forward. Rachel spotted Ruth Gruber among them. She was looking through her camera and snapping pictures of the disturbance. A man, his shirt soaked with blood, tried to show the reporter his wounds. Two soldiers dragged him away. Other soldiers pulled people by their hair and rolled passengers down the gangway like barrels. Meanwhile music blared from a loudspeaker.

"They're trying to hide the sound of people screaming," Rachel exclaimed.

"It's not working," Hensche said in a disgusted voice.

A man being hauled off by soldiers shrieked, "They shall not keep us from our homeland!"

"Rachel!" Her mother yanked her forward. "Let's go."

Rachel stumbled as they moved toward British soldiers who were directing them to a waiting train. It was an old train with all the seats ripped out. The windows were securely shut with bars and iron mesh. Rachel sat on the floor with her knees pulled up and her chin resting on her hands. Miriam sat beside her. Her mother and Hensche remained standing in the crowded car. When it was packed full, the soldiers slammed the door. The whistle blasted and the train lurched forward.

THE TERRORIST IS COMING TO CARNE[GIE] —Story on p[age]

THE ANSWER

THE STRUGGLE FOR HEBREW NATIONAL INDEPENDENCE OF PALESTINE

AN AMERICAN WEEKLY DEDICATED TO LIBERATION AND THE

TEN CENTS

FRIDAY, SEPTEMBER 12, 1947

VOL. V No. 37

Journal NEW YORK American

British Club Jews to Force Them to Land in Hamburg

New York World-Telegram

DEFIANT JEWS BATTERED, HOSED, CARTED OFF THIRD REFUGEE SHIP

New York Post

British Club Jews Resisting Landing At Hamburg—'Hitlerism,' They Cry

Hamburg, Sept. 8 (AP)—The British Government today landed 1,206 of the Exodus 1947 Jews it barred from Palestine, but only after soldiers had clubbed or flailed scores who resisted a loudspeaker invitation to step peacefully onto German soil.

NEW YORK Herald Tribune

1,406 Exodus Jews Landed, Some Clubbed

Two-thirds of Refugees Debark Quietly, Young Men Resist Below Deck

Four-Hour Struggle Seen by Reporters

Jews Interned in Camp Near Hamburg; Second Vessel Unloads Today

By Marguerite Higgins

Club-Wielding Red Devils Clear Last of Exodus Lot After Bloody Hold Battle

'Fascists, Beasts!' Refugees Shriek as Tommies Push Some Ashore at Hamburg

The Sun

Screams of 'Hitlerism' Go Up as Troo[ps] Club Many Refugees Refusing to Quit the Ocean Vigour.

Britons Club Jews at Hamburg

Resisting Refugees Carried Ashore Bodily, Hoses Out at D.P. Camp.

Hamburg, Sept. 8 (A.P.)—British soldiers swingin[g]

Scores of Resisters Ashore and Are Tak[en] Detention Cam[p]

'HEIL HITLER' RISES IN LONDON STREETS

Police Break Up Veterans' Meeting as Prats Calls for Throttling of Fascists

LONDON, Sept. 7 (P)—Cries of "Heil Hitler" sounded in the streets of London's slum district day while a few British prais[e]...

Troops Wield Clubs, Hoses British Drag Refugees Off Ship at Dock

HAMBURG, Sept. 8 (AP)—The British Go[v]ernment landed today 1,206 of the Exodus 1947 J[e]ws it barred from Palestine, but only after soldiers ha[d] clubbed or flailed scores who resisted a loud-speak[er] invitation to step peacefully onto German soil.
Cries of "this is Hitlerism" came from the Jews as [...]

SDAY, SEPTEMBER 9, 1947

PM THE WORLD

500 Jews Reported Beaten By British

By MAURICE PEARLMAN

HAMBURG

Some 500 of the 1,406 Ocean Vigour refugees barred by being British troops from the landing...

Dance Music Blares Out

The remainder of the refugees seemed to go down the gang group once they had been brought from the holds on to the deck.

While this "Operation Oust," as the Army terms it, was going on, a loud speaker blared forth the...

TOKEN FIGHT AS JEWS OF [...] BEGIN DEBA[...]

[...] Hurt as Jews Of Vessel and Clubs Spank[...]

The New York T[...]

NO STORY

Since no story can do justice to the horrors described

CHAPTER 28

In the Displaced
Persons Camp

The *Exodus* refugees were taken to three DP camps: Emden, Poppendorf, and Am Stau. Rachel and her family were sent to Am Stau. Her first impression of the camp was that it was yet another prison. Again, they were behind a barbed wire fence. Armed soldiers in tall guard towers watched them from above. The refugees were locked inside with no way to get out. Conditions were poor. They lived with no heat, thirty people to a hut. By the end of September it was getting cold.

Although the authorities tried to keep the refugees ignorant of what was happening in the outside world, news crept into the camp. They learned that on the night they had arrived in Hamburg, thousands of fellow Holocaust survivors from a neighboring DP camp

The Exodus *refugees were loaded
into trucks to be taken to several
Displaced Person camps.*

had gathered to protest, bearing signs that read: "*Exodus* refugees, we come to you united in the struggle for free immigration to Palestine."

Rachel, Miriam, and Saul were sitting on Rachel's bunk, wrapped in blankets. The structure where they lived was a long wooden building with a corrugated metal roof. The wind whistled through the cracks between the wooden boards.

"I heard they're going to move us to another camp," Saul told them.

Rachel was happy that Saul was with them in Am Stau. David, who had been on the *Runnymede Park,* had been sent to Poppendorf.

"Where are you getting your information now? We don't have chocolate to trade in here," Rachel asked.

"I keep my ears open."

"I hope they decide soon." Rachel shivered.

Once again Rachel and her mother and sister packed their belongings. Now all the refugees from the *Exodus* were to be housed in Emden and Sengwarden. The Landesman family was sent to Sengwarden. Fortunately, Sengwarden was a former naval base and the living conditions were more comfortable. Here the refugees were free to leave the camp. And instead of wooden huts, they lived in a room in a brick building with a small wood stove to keep them warm and to heat up food.

A school was set up for the children. There were also classes for the adults in agriculture, mechanics, sewing, and other trades so that people would be able to find work wherever they landed. Secretly, members of the Haganah were teaching young adults other skills. They were training them to be soldiers in case they needed to defend their new home, once they got there. Hensche was in one of the groups led by Aviva who traveled between the Sengwarden and Emden camps for the training sessions.

Rachel was delighted to be back at school. She studied, learned to ride a bicycle, and spent time with Miriam and Saul. But like everyone else in the camp, she considered her life there temporary. While they waited for a change in the British immigration policy, they discussed their future plans – Miriam hoped to become a nurse, Rachel a teacher – and prepared for the day when they would be allowed to legally enter Eretz Yisroel. The rumor was that it might happen soon.

"You weren't in class today." Rachel gave Saul a questioning look. "Did you sneak into the training camp again?"

They were standing outside Sengwarden's main building. During the day, it was their school. At night, it became a social hall, and on Friday nights and Saturdays, it was the synagogue.

"Yes," Saul said in a defiant voice. Then his tone softened. "I don't want to fight. But if I have to, in order to protect our new country, I will. I don't ever want to live in fear, like we did during the war."

Saul turned and walked away from them, on his way back to the training camp.

CHAPTER 29

The United Nations Votes

November 29, 1947

The plight of the *Exodus* refugees had indeed attracted worldwide attention with pictures of Jews being clubbed and dragged off the ships. The fact that Britain had sent Holocaust survivors back to Germany had raised outrage. It was this attention that the refugees hoped would influence the United Nations (UN) to vote in favor of dividing Palestine into two states, one of them to become a home for Jews.

The United Nations was formed in 1945 after World War II ended. It was an organization with representatives from countries around the world who met to work out international issues instead of going to war over them. The fate of Palestine was such an issue.

In January 1947, Britain informed the UN that it wished to end its control of Palestine and would pull its army out in May 1948. It was now up to the member countries of the UN to vote on whether or not to grant the Jews a place of refuge in that part of the world.

Rachel knew about the upcoming vote because it was all the adults were talking about. As the day for the vote drew near, tension in the camp built up to a fever pitch. Would there be two states? One that would be for Arab Palestinians and one for Jews, who would finally have a safe place to call home? What would the members of the UN decide?

Finally, the day arrived. The voting session was broadcast from the UN internationally, including in Germany. Everyone in the camp crowded into the main building. They huddled around a radio and listened to the news from UN headquarters in New York City.

Rachel closed her eyes. She was so nervous that she could hardly breathe. *This is the most important moment of my life. This vote will decide if we will have a safe home.* She felt a hand on her arm. She turned and saw her sister looking at her. Wordlessly, they listened as the voting began.

Someone had wheeled a blackboard into the room. Rachel's English teacher stood with a piece of white chalk, ready to record the votes as they came in. "Quiet everyone." She held up her hand. "The voting has begun." As the countries' votes came in, she recorded each one on the board.

Afghanistan: No
Canada: Yes
Greece: No
Argentina: Abstain

"What does abstain mean?" Rachel asked her mother.

"It means that the country does not want to vote either yes or no. Shh." She shushed her daughter as the voting continued.

France: Yes

"France voted for us," another man exclaimed.

"Shah! I can't hear the voting," a woman hissed.

Australia: Yes
The United States: Yes
Cuba: No
Belgium: Yes
Pakistan: No
India: No
China: Abstain
Iran: No
Peru: Yes
Egypt: No
Czechoslovakia: Yes

Iraq: No
Lebanon: No
Denmark: Yes

The resolution needed 31 votes to pass. Rachel stood with her friends and they kept score. Each time there was a No vote the room seemed to freeze and hold its breath. Each Yes ignited a spark of hope.

"We're nearly there," Saul said, " but almost all the countries have already sent in their votes," he added, looking worried. "We still need one more."

Honduras: Abstain
Yemen: No

"The Philippines votes Yes," the voice on the radio announced.

"That's it! Thirty-one! It passed." Rachel jumped up and down. She hugged Miriam. Miriam hugged Saul who kept, repeating over and over: "We will have our own country."

All around them people were laughing, crying, kissing and hugging. They barely heard the rest of the votes.

"Mama!" Rachel kissed her mother and then looked for Hensche. She was with a group of young people her age dancing a *hora*. Rachel and Miriam ran over and joined them. They linked arms, singing and dancing. Their joy exploded like fireworks lighting up the night.

Rachel, center, made friends at the camp, where they all went to training sessions to prepare for their new lives.

CHAPTER 30
A Celebration of Life

After the excitement of the UN vote, life in the refugee camp settled back into a routine. The *Exodus* refugees knew now that once the British left Palestine in May, they would be able to legally enter the new country. While they waited, they tried to put the past behind them and start to rebuild their lives.

Rachel continued her classes, Hensche was taking a sewing class, and Mama, who was an excellent seamstress, was working in the camp's clothing department, repairing old garments.

The weather had turned bitterly cold. But thanks to the efforts of international relief organizations, the refugees were well fed and warm. Rachel received second-hand clothes – skirts, sweaters, coats, shoes – from North America, but they were new to her. She often thought of the girls who had worn them and she thanked them in her heart for sharing.

The refugees came together to celebrate the Jewish holidays as if they were one large family. And almost every week there was a wedding or the birth of a new baby.

"Why are so many people getting married?" Rachel asked her mother one day. Mama was sewing a bridal veil for a young woman who was getting married the following week.

"People who have lost their families are anxious to begin new ones," her mother replied. She had a faraway look in her eyes. Rachel knew she was thinking of her father. *Miriam says that I am lucky because I have my mother and two sisters. And she is right. But we have lost family too. I don't talk about Papa because it is too painful. But I miss him every day.*

"Mama, will you ever get married again?"

"Rachel!" Her mother waved her hand, brushing her question away. "What makes you ask such a thing?"

Rachel gave her a sly grin. "Everyone else is doing it."

"Don't you have homework to keep that mind of yours busy?"

"Yes, Mama." She jumped to her feet. "I have to study my Hebrew."

"So, go. I have work to do."

Rachel left her mother to her sewing and walked outside. A woman who had been pregnant on the *Exodus* was pushing a baby carriage.

"Hello, Mrs. Posner. May I see the baby?"

Smiling, the woman pulled back the blanket to reveal a chubby baby in a blue sweater and matching bonnet.

Rachel bent over and slipped her finger into his fisted hand. He clutched it and smiled. "He is beautiful!"

"Yes." The baby's mother bent down and adjusted his blanket. "He is my joy and our future. Now, I must take Benjamin inside to feed him. *Shalom,* Rachel."

"*Shalom,* Mrs. Posner."

As she walked to her room, Rachel thought about what Mrs. Posner had said. Each newborn *was* the future, a sign that life would continue. After sharing many hardships aboard the ships, the refugees continued to celebrate and dream about the future. They talked all the time about finally going to a safe home and they made plans for what they would do once they got there.

What they didn't talk about was the lost parents and children, aunts, uncles, and cousins who had been murdered by the Nazis. They didn't talk about what they had seen and heard in the concentration camps. They seldom talked about what they themselves had experienced in the war. Those subjects were too painful to voice aloud. So they lived, ate, played games, sang, and staged performances in the camp. And waited to go to the land that would give them shelter, a place they could finally call home.

PART FOUR
A New Home

Palestine Post, May 14, 1948

CHAPTER 31
The Jewish State of Israel

May 14, 1948

Warm air drifted through the open window. The long, cold winter was finally over and once again, everyone was gathered around the radio. The British were leaving Palestine the following day and anticipation was growing.

Now, six months after the UN vote, everyone was waiting for David Ben-Gurion, leader of the Jewish government in Palestine, to address the world. What would he say? The room was silent. The only sound was the ticking of the clock on the wall and the static crackles from the radio. And then Ben-Gurion began to speak:

"It is the natural right of a people to be as any other nation. Self-reliant and in their own state. By virtue of our natural and historic right, and based on the UN resolution, we hereby declare the establishment of a Jewish state in the Land of Israel, which will be called the State of Israel."

The room erupted in shouts and cheers. Rachel touched her face. Her cheeks were wet.

"Rachel, it has happened." Miriam grabbed her hands and spun her round and round. Others joined them. They linked arms and started to dance, even as Ben-Gurion continued his speech.

And then, everyone stopped. From the radio came the strains of an orchestra playing "Hatikvah." Together, in voices strong and loud, the refugees joined in, singing their new anthem.

Next time I sing "Hatikvah," Rachel thought, *I will sing it in Israel.*

CHAPTER 32
Departure for Israel

The United States was the first country to officially recognize the State of Israel. Others soon followed. The refugees were ecstatic. Now they could go there freely without having to be smuggled through British blockades.

"As Jews, we will automatically become Israeli citizens." Rachel couldn't contain her excitement. With hundreds of thousands of refugees ready to go to Israel, the Landesmans had to wait their turn. Miriam had already left with a group of orphans. Rachel missed her, but hoped she would see her again in Israel. Saul was gone too.

Then one day, in July 1948, Rachel's mother told her that they were leaving by train for Marseilles and from there would travel by ship to Israel.

"Batya says it will not be easy," her mother said. She had received a letter from Batya telling them that life in Israel was hard.

"What else does she say?"

"She says that it's a new country with many problems. People work very hard. There are so many refugees like us that there is a shortage of housing. The government is rationing food and clothing to make sure that there is enough for everyone."

"Does that mean we will be hungry?"

"No, Rachel," Hensche said. "It means that we will eat with thought and not waste anything."

"That won't be a problem." Their mother gave them a sour look. "We have been living like that for many years."

"During the war there were times we had no food. That won't happen in Israel, will it?" Rachel turned to Hensche.

"Absolutely not," Hensche assured her. "We are going there at a very exciting time. Imagine, we are going to help build a brand new country."

❀ ❀ ❀

Rachel helped her mother and Hensche pack their belongings. Finally they were going to the place they had dreamed about for such a long time. Rachel looked around the room where they had lived for the last eight months. *I'm not sorry to leave,* she thought. *Whatever hardships we face in Israel will be worth it. We're going to have a home at last where we will feel safe and free.* She smiled a great big happy smile.

CHAPTER 33
The Final Voyage

August 20, 1948

Once again, the Landesmans were aboard a ship, this time the SS *Kedmah*. Conditions on this ship were luxurious compared to the *Exodus* or the *Ocean Vigour*. Rachel, her mother and Hensche had a cabin all to themselves. It had proper beds and a private bathroom. There was a wide deck where passengers could walk or sit on the wooden deck chairs and enjoy the sun and ocean air. When Rachel looked up, she saw blue Stars of David painted on the ship's funnel. There was a social lounge and a dining room and all the food was kosher. Even nature did its part. The weather was good and the sea was calm during the entire trip.

As the ship neared Haifa, Rachel stood at the rail feeling relief.

There were no soldiers with guns, no barbed wire. She reached into her pocket and pulled out the coin Avram had given her. *Spend it in Eretz Yisroel*, he had said.

"I will, Avram," she whispered into the air.

She looked at the people on the shore. Most of them were there to welcome friends and relatives arriving on the ship. They were waving and cheering. Rachel wished that Batya and her husband had been able to be there to meet them, but she knew they would be reunited soon. Rachel waved back to the crowd. "*Shalom!*" she called out.

Because it was the Sabbath, the passengers had to wait until sunset to disembark. Rachel was so restless she could hardly stand still. Her mother and Hensche were resting in their cabin. As usual, Rachel was on deck. She didn't want to miss a minute of their arrival.

At last, the sun was setting. Rachel watched as the sky turned from blue to the palest pink, then a deeper peach, and finally a fiery orange. Looking up, she saw the first star. *Shabbat* was over. It was time to leave the *Kedmah*.

No one escorted them or tried to push them as they walked down the gangplank. They left the ship quietly and peacefully, carrying their belongings. As they stepped onto the dock in Haifa, Rachel looked up at Mount Carmel and remembered the last time she had stood there, surrounded by armed British soldiers. That time, the winking lights in the houses on the hill had filled her with sadness. This time they called to her. She could almost hear them saying, *Rachel Landesman, welcome home.*

Mount Carmel

AUTHOR'S NOTE

The Ship to Nowhere is a true story. Rachel, her sister and mother are real people who made the treacherous journey on the *Exodus 1947*. So are Captain Ike, Yossi Harel, Bill Bernstein, Ruth Gruber, and Mordecai Rosman. Other characters such as Rachel's friends Miriam, Saul, and David represent the people she met on the *Exodus*. Aviva and Avram represent the many Haganah men and women who organized and ran the movement of illegal ships that tried to break through the British blockade. When Israel became a state, the Haganah became the Israeli army, today known as the Israel Defense Force.

Rachel Landesman was one of the 4,500 Jewish refugees crowded on board the *Exodus 1947*. She, her sister, and their mother had barely survived the Holocaust in Czechoslovakia and later in Hungary.

After the war, the family lived in a series of Displaced Persons camps. Through all of these trials, Rachel had one wish: To leave intolerance and war behind and live in a land where she would feel safe to be a Jew.

This book ends with Rachel and her family arriving in Israel in 1948. Of course, their story did not stop there. As they had been warned, life in Israel was difficult. The new country was struggling to absorb more than 350,000 new immigrants from the camps in Europe and from other countries. Food and clothing were in short supply and were rationed to make sure there was enough to go around and no one went hungry. When they arrived, Rachel's family went to an absorption center for new immigrants where they learned about the country and how to read, write, and speak Hebrew. From there, Hensche went into the army, as did most of the young men and women. While her mother looked for work and a place to live, Rachel was taken in by an organization that cared for children who were Holocaust survivors. She remained there while she finished elementary school and then went to high school. When she was 16, Rachel moved to Jerusalem to attend teachers' college. In 1956, at the age of 18, her sister Batya, who had meanwhile moved with her husband to Toronto, Canada, sent her a ticket to come and visit them.

Rachel met and married her husband, Chaim, in Canada and they had two sons. Rachel's mother remarried and remained in Israel until her death. Hensche also remained in Israel, married and had a family.

In 2012, Rachel and her husband moved to Israel to be near their sons, who were married and living in Israel with their families. Today Rachel lives in Jerusalem, the city of gold that she dreamed of as a young girl on a crowded ship running the British blockade.

As for Captain Ike, he later started his own shipping company in Israel. He married and had two daughters. In 1958 he went to the US where he earned degrees in economics and international relations. Back in Israel, he built his dream home, shaped like a ship and overlooking the sea. He died there in 1993 at the age of 86.

Rachel's late husband Chaim, center, and her sons Tsvi, left, and Boaz, right.

Ruth Gruber followed the story of the *Exodus* refugees from Tel Aviv to Haifa, then to Cyprus, where the three prison ships failed to arrive, then to Marseilles, and finally to Hamburg, where she wrote about the brutal treatment of refugees on the dock. In 1948 she wrote a book called *Exodus 1947* about her experiences and the plight of the *Exodus* passengers.

Ruth Gruber went on to write many more books and receive numerous awards for her fearless reporting on important issues. She lives in New York City and at the time of this writing is 105 years old. When asked for the secret of her success she once replied, "Have dreams, have visions, and let no obstacle stop you."

And what about the *Exodus 1947*? After its historic voyage, the badly damaged ship was moored just offshore from Haifa, ignored and forgotten. In 1950 the mayor of Haifa attempted to have the ship restored and turned into a museum about the illegal immigration of Jews to Palestine. There was an accident during the restoration, however, and the *Exodus* burned down to her waterline. Later the wreck was sunk and today a modern concrete quay for cargo ships in Haifa's port lies atop the remains of the unlikely ship that sailed into history with its cargo of hopes and dreams.

ACKNOWLEDGMENTS

This has been an amazing and exciting book to write. First, I want to thank Rachel Fletcher (her married name) for allowing me to tell her story. I met her through my friend Dinah Gruber. When I heard Rachel's story, I knew I had to write it. Rachel and the passengers on *Exodus 1947* had the conviction and courage to realize their dream and they enabled hundreds of thousands of others to do the same.

I am indebted to Margie Wolfe and her team at Second Story Press for believing in this book and working with me to bring it to fruition. My editor Sarah Swartz provided much needed insight and invaluable guidance.

I want to thank the Ontario Arts Council for its support. The saga of the Haganah ship *Exodus 1947* has become famous, but few people know the full story. I learned a great deal in researching the book and I'm delighted for the opportunity to share it with my readers.

—Rona Arato

The Haganah leaders realized that the *Exodus 1947* was an historic endeavor. They issued certificates to everyone who had been on board, so that in years to come, only those who were actually on board the ship could claim to have been part of the journey.

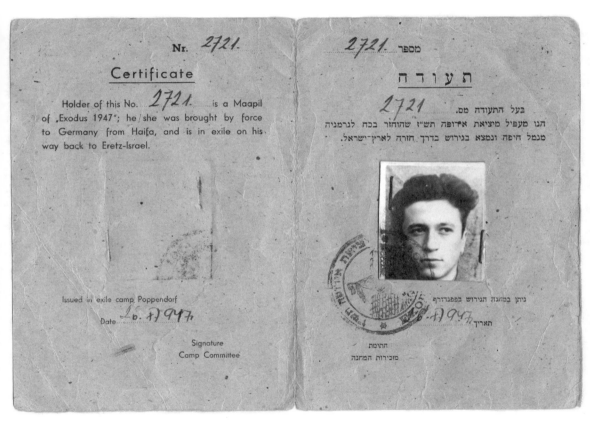

Certificate issued by the Haganah to everyone who was on the ship Exodus 1947.

SOURCES AND BIBLIOGRAPHY

[1] Gruber, Ruth. *Exodus 1947: The Ship That Launched a Nation*. New York: Times Books, Random House, 1948, p.45

[2] Ibid, p.46

[3] Ibid, p.51

Hagenah Ship 'Exodus' – 5707, by Dov Frieberg, jewishgen.org website.

Stars and Stripes, Joe Fleming and William B. Lee, Steptember 9, 1947

The United States Holocaust Memorial Museum: www.ushmm.org
www.machal.org.i./index.php?

http://archives.chicagotribune.com/1947/09/08/page/12/article/
fog-in-hamburg-hides-fate-of-refugee-jews

http://collections.ushmm.org/search/catalog/pa1117546

http://www.truppenuebungsplatzbergen.com/hawti6.htm

http://bcrfj.revues.org/269

http://www.historama.com/online-resources/articles/israel/story_
israel_first_independence_day_14_may_1948.html

PHOTO CREDITS

Page 50: Courtesy of the Central Zionist Archives, Jerusalem

Page 64: United States Holocaust Memorial Museum, courtesy of Murray T. Aronoff

Page 67: United States Holocaust Memorial Museum, courtesy of Bernard Marks

Page 74: United States Holocaust Memorial Museum, courtesy of Avi Livney

Page 75: ACME Photo, courtesy of Yad Vashem

Page 76: (top) ACME Photo, courtesy of Yad Vashem (bottom) United States Holocaust Memorial Museum, courtesy of the Israel Government Press Office

Page 80: (top) Courtesy of the Central Zionist Archives, Jerusalem (bottom) United States Holocaust Memorial Museum, courtesy of Murray T. Aronoff

Page 118: United States Holocaust Memorial Museum, courtesy of Marion Michel Oliner

Page 128: Yad Vashem

Page 129: Yad Vashem

Page 132: United States Holocaust Memorial Museum, courtesy of Murray T. Aronoff

Page 134: Yad Vashem

Page 142: Courtesy Rachel Fletcher

Page 143: Courtesy Rachel
Fletcher

Page 159: Courtesy Rachel
Fletcher

Page 163: United States
Holocaust Memorial Museum,
courtesy of Chanina and Sara
Kam

ABOUT THE AUTHOR

Rona Arato, a former teacher with a passion for human rights, is the award-winning author of 20 children's books including *The Last Train, a Holocaust Story*. She was an interviewer for *Survivors of the Shoah*, a Steven Spielberg project that recorded histories of Holocaust survivors. She lives in Toronto.